The Way of the Accidental Entrepreneur

How to Grow a Business that Fits Just-Right

you

Molly Molly Gordon

Shaboom **!** Inc.

Suquamish Washington USA
www.shaboominc.com

Published by Shaboom ! Inc.
PO Box 195
Suquamish, WA 98392 USA
360-697-7022
www.shaboominc.com
mgordon@shaboominc.com

Dedicated to Miles Yanick,
my husband and Charming Prince.
Life with you *is* a dream...

Acknowledgments

Writing this book has been an exercise in receiving support and guidance. More people have contributed to the process than I can name. If you are one of them and are not named here, please forgive my oversight and consider yourself deeply appreciated.

Chief among the contributors to this book is Jude Spacks, whose deft editorial hand made the book immeasurably better. I declared the text complete against editorial advice, though with her gracious support. Any gaps, confusing bits, or typos are entirely my own.

Thank you to Maggie Haydock, my invaluable assistant and beloved sister. Maggie makes coming to work a joy even when I don't want to run into my boss (who would be me). Debbie Buxton has been my virtual assistant for almost 10 years, keeping the Web site and newsletter in order, in spite of my unpredictable course corrections. Thank you for putting up with me, Deb.

Then there are the members of the Brain Trust: Jennifer Louden, Michael Bungay Stanier, Michele Christensen, and Mark Silver. Everyone of them played a key role in the process. Special thanks to Mark for getting me to write the book and to Michael for telling the story of the boids at our retreat.

Thanks to the members of the Monday morning Mastermind group: Bob Linz, Marit Saltrones, Kevin Dwyer, John Ellis, and David Hager for months of encouragement and the reminder not to get wrapped around the axle. Donna Zajonc and David Womeldorff were also great role models for staying with the process.

The list of family and friends who tolerated broken dates, postponed get-togethers, and distracted conversations is too long to print. Thanks, guys, I'm back. (Uh oh!)

About the Illustrator

Sean D' Souza didn't speak much when he was growing up. But he found that cartoons were a good way to get people to speak to him. Through school, his friends remembered him for his illustrations, and by the time he was in university, he was using cartoons as his 'chick magnet.' He also found he could get paid for cartoons along the line and has drawn for several newspapers, magazines and big-name (and small companies) worldwide.

Sean now lives in New Zealand, and his work can be seen at www.psychotactics.com/cartoon.

Table of Contents

Introduction

Of all the crooked paths I have taken, self-employment has been the most challenging and enriching. Every day that I work for myself is a day I come face to face with—well, with me. Sometimes that's really fun, sometimes it verges on the horrific. It is always educational. ☺

This book tells the story of how I grew a successful coaching business. For me, success means earning enough money without being obsessed with it, enjoying the people I work with, and getting to use my own life as a laboratory where my experiments, and sometimes accidents, are useful to my clients and customers.

The best thing and worst thing about working for myself is that everything is connected. I don't need to be someone different at work than I am in the rest of my life. What I learn in either area serves me (and I hope others) in both.

Working for myself also means that everything is distorted through the projector that is my mind. That's not a problem, at least not when I remember that Reality is always kinder than any stressful thoughts I have about it. As you will see, this realization is at the core of the Way of the Accidental Entrepreneur.

Before You Begin

If you are like me, you are anxious to improve your business or to start a business that will succeed. Boy, do I get that. At the same time, please stop right now to read these few important rules of the road. It will save you heaps of time and probably heaps of money. It will certainly shorten your learning curve.

This is not a get-rich-quick book. It is a be-successful-now book. If you accept the premise that self-employment is a spiritual or personal growth path, you are already "there." As you apply the principles and use the tools in this book, all sorts of things will happen including, I believe, the cultivation of a business that fits you just-right. Still, you will be no more successful when your business is thriving than you are now. At every step you will only have the present moment in which to thrive.

I know that's pretty abstract, and most of the time I forget it myself. But it is the foundation of this book and the basis for everything good that has happened to me. As a dear friend likes to say, "Everything good that has ever happened to me came in spite of my efforts. Everything that has gone wrong has my fingerprints all over it."

This leads straight to the paradox that while it's up to us to do the work of waking up, what that looks like and how it happens is none of our business. Again, I forget that a lot. Still, if there is a "secret" to my success, it is showing up over and over again to take the next indicated step and letting go of the results.

What to Expect

This book gives you tools to grow your business in a certain Way, the Way of the Accidental Entrepreneur. By following the Three Instructions that make up that Way, you will gain confidence in yourself and in the gift you are. You may also experience disappointment, frustration, and even anger, but these will be temporary so long as you come back to the Way.

I don't know how to stay on a diet, balance my checkbook every month, or meditate every day. I've never been consistent in anything except that I have always been utterly fascinated with life. From the time I was a little girl, I would sometimes hear myself when I argued with Reality. Sooner or later, I'd stop fighting. Then, when I surrendered, I would get so excited that I had to tell the world. "Hey, everybody! The only person in the way of my happiness is me! Is that cool, or what?"

Your mileage may vary. ☺

December, 2007
Suquamish, Washington

Psst... Bug Alert

Lots of people have worked hard to make sure this book is letter-perfect, and it's a good bet that we've missed a few things. If you find a typo, misspelling, or anything that just plain bugs you, tell us. Email the details (page number, for example, so we can fix things) to maggie@shaboominc.com. We'll not only use your feedback in the second edition, you could win a prize for the best bug.

Getting Clear

Be patient toward all that is unsolved in your heart and try to love the questions themselves like locked rooms and like books that are written in a very foreign tongue. Do not now seek the answers, which cannot be given you because you would not be able to live them. And the point is, to live everything. Live the questions now. Perhaps you will find them gradually, without noticing it, and live along some distant day into the answer. ~Rainer Maria Rilke

Chapter 1

A Is for Accidental

I will never forget my first A. My mom and grandparents were ecstatic. We called my dad, who was serving in the Air Force in Saudi Arabia, to share the good news. I still have the scrap of paper on which he recorded my grades that day. Nothing I had done before this had produced such stunning approval.

Naturally, I wanted more, and from second grade through high school, I got As and the occasional B. If I got a C along the way, I have succeeded in repressing the memory. (My college grades were either As or Fs, and that's another story.)

All of this is to say that I love to be right. Imagine my surprise when I encountered Real Life.

Revolution

In real life, you don't get As. Deprived of my primary source of security and self-esteem, I became a self-styled revolutionary. This was revolution 1970s style: passionate, self-absorbed, clear about what needed to go (war, the establishment, plastic*) and foggy about what would replace it. Materialism was bad. Corporations were evil. Power to the people! If I couldn't be right, by God, I'd be righteous.

---

* *Plastic* was used as a derogatory term for all that was inauthentic, phony, unnatural, and dishonest, and we who opposed it were confident in our ability to distinguish the real from the false.

The strategy of being right when I could and a bad-girl when I couldn't ran my life well into the 80s. Actually, they ran it into the ground, though I'm not complaining. By March 1984 I was teetering over the cutting edge of poly-addiction. By the end of April, I was a poster-child for recovery. (Being a good girl works well when you're institutionalized.)

Gainful Employment

By 1986 I was working for a small advocacy organization with an international base. I edited the newsletter, gave administrative support to their boards and committees, and learned to make my tiny Kaypro computer do back flips. Things were looking up.

And then they looked down. I had a spat with the Executive Director and gave notice. Now I joke and call this the first sign that I was becoming psychologically unemployable.

Mollycoddles

I had been a compulsive knitter throughout the early years of recovery, whipping out a sweater a week during the twice-daily ferry and bus commute. The incessant knitting (while smoking, reading, and drinking coffee, no less) attracted attention. I liked that. A few people told me I should sell my work. Flattery took me by the nose and led me down the garden path, not that I put up much of a fight.

I decided to be an artist when I grew up. I started selling my work in 1987 and in 1989 became the full time proprietor of Mollycoddles, a wearable art studio. I have always loved the limelight, and I have a flair for getting attention, so getting known for my work was easy. I was recognized in national magazines, invited to the better craft shows, and taught creativity and color work at knitting conferences.

Bitten by a Niche

While I was basking in the glow of recognition, I noticed that most of my fellow artists were clueless about self-promotion. I've never been able to keep what I think I know to myself, so in 1993

I applied for and received a grant to do a workshop, "Business Communications for Artists and Artisans." It went extremely well, and people—even non-artists—began phoning me for business advice.

I was not a happy camper. Mollycoddles was barely paying its bills, let alone paying me. I wanted to sell sweaters, not help daycare providers and music teachers with their business problems. I told people I didn't do business consulting and sent them away, muttering that they should know better than to waste my time and why didn't they buy a sweater? (So much for recognizing my niche.)

This continued until September 1995, when I experienced a blinding flash of the obvious (BFO): after eight years I still wasn't making money, and it had stopped being fun. I decided to close the studio at the end of the year without having any idea about what I would do instead.

The decision to close Mollycoddles without an alternate plan wasn't as risky as it sounds. I'd been losing money steadily, and the truth was we'd be ahead financially the minute I shut the doors.

Still, I did need to come up with a game plan. This was when I realized that I might actually be psychologically unemployable. Scary as self-employment is and unsuccessful as I had been in my first venture, I could not see myself walking into an office building or commuting ever again.

Just Say Yes

I decided I would start saying yes to people who called for business support. I told a few people I was going to help people who liked their work but didn't know how to run a business (as if I did!). In a matter of weeks I had six clients, and I was so terrified that I would be busted as an impostor, I stopped talking about my work.

I proceeded to work 14 hours a day for those six clients, desperately trying to justify the $35 an hour I charged them. I created databases for one client, designed a poster for another, and wrote brochures, press releases, and even business policies. I only billed my clients for the hour a week we spent face-to-face, feeling that the behind the scenes work was something I owed them to validate the plans and choices they made when we talked.

Here's the math. I saw an average of four clients each week. Four times $35 = $140. I was making about $2.00 an hour. I was exhausted. Bizarrely, I was worried sick that I wasn't delivering good value to my clients. (Oh, by the way, I let one of my clients run up a $540 bill because I didn't think it was fair to strain her operating budget, despite the fact that my help was what kept her business from falling apart.)

I confided my worries to one of my clients, who was also a good friend. I told her I hadn't a clue what people really wanted from me or how to identify the value they got from our conversations. She reassured me that she was getting her money's worth, but she couldn't explain how, at least not in terms I understood.

A few weeks later she sent me a *Newsweek* article about coaching. Above the headline was a sticky note that said this was what she thought I was doing. I devoured the article, then read it again. I jumped online and learned everything I could about this new field. Some of it struck me as glib and over-rated, but mostly it felt like coming home. So I became a coach.

Right and Wrong Revisited

I often marvel at how much I did right in the first three years of my coaching business, especially since most of it went against conventional wisdom. I continued to read everything I could find about the field, and I just couldn't bring myself to build a business the way coaches were being advised to in those days.

For one thing, there was no way I was going to go from charging $35 an hour to $300/month (for 3 or 4 coaching calls), which was touted as a reasonable going rate for a beginning coach. Instead, I played with some figures and arrived at $175 a month for four one-hour sessions. I figured that, including email, this would amount to about $50 an hour. That was a stretch, but one I could make without freaking myself out.

I built my own Web site, but it didn't look anything like the Web sites other coaches had. I wasn't comfortable making the kinds of claims other coaches were making, so I mostly talked about who I was, what I liked, and what I was learning.

I also didn't have a business plan, though that wasn't for lack of trying. I drafted plan after plan, creating one scenario after another, yet none of them gelled. After six or seven tries, I noticed that I would get sick—physically ill or depressed—every time I labored over a business plan. Finally, I swore off writing business plans and decided to just listen to my one remaining client.

That's right. Among the paradoxical results of getting clear about what I had to offer was this: within a month or so of declaring myself a coach, I let my existing clients go. By not knowing what value I was providing, undercharging, and over-performing, I had turned each of these perfectly lovely people into an energy drain. Through no fault of their own, they had become dependent on my support instead of strengthened by it.

Letting go of the wrong clients meant getting my first just-right client, a client who thrived in our relationship. She hired me as a coach, not a rescuer. I adored working with her because she knew what she wanted; she knew how to make it work for her; and delivering value to her was a slam dunk for me. I decided that the most important thing I could do to grow my business was to listen to her and find out what she got from our work together.

Goals That Fit Just-Right

That took care of some pieces of a business plan like "What is my market?" (people like her) and "What do I do for them?"

(clarify choices, reflect priorities and values). The next step was to set goals.

At the time everything I was reading about starting a business and about coaching said you should set audacious goals. That felt right. I absolutely wanted a goal I cared about, a goal I could feel my innards stretching toward like a sunflower follows the sun.

At the same time, something in me balked when I would try on the kind of impressive goals that I thought I should set, like earning six figures in 12 months or filling my clients list in six. And then it hit me: the most audacious goal I could set was the goal of having a business that fit me just-right. How audacious is that? (You're supposed to say, "Why, Molly, that is *very* audacious. Good for you!)

For me, a business that fit just-right would earn a six-figure income, but in three to five years, not one. It would have a full client list—but one filled by clients who fit, clients who felt like they knew me before they hired me. Having clients like that takes time.

I decided then that having a just-right business was my first priority. This took heaps of pressure off because now I was the authority on what my business should look and feel like. I could get excited about growing a business I actually wanted, and I could trust myself to stay the course.

I set out to get six clients in my first year of practice. (Six clients @ $175 = $1050 per month. Not exactly princely.) My plan was to double that in the second year and again in the third. It worked. I got my fifth and sixth clients on the last day of the first year.

Within three years, I had a full practice and an email newsletter with 1200 subscribers (up from the first 45 victims to whom I sent the first issues without troubling to ask their permission. Please, do as I say, not as I did.). But you should also know that, at one point in the second year, I was down to two clients. I realized that to be true to my audacious goal of a business that fit just-right, I would need to pay attention to the overall trend and not get distracted by temporary ups and downs. Since I'd had six clients once, I would have them—and more—again.

Time and distance turned Mollycoddles into a thorough business education. Two years after closing the doors, my mistakes and blind spots had begun to morph into understanding. I had accidentally become a reasonably successful entrepreneur.

Chapter 2

Good Things Happen by Accident

The most important thing I can tell you about how I became a successful coach is that I cooperated with accident. I read the books that interested me, which invariably turned out to be helpful to my clients. When I had more time than money, a common circumstance in the early days of being in business, I used my time to learn my way around the Internet. I played with various software programs. Sometimes I simply used the extra time to rest or to enjoy myself—imagine!

Paying Dues

Cooperating with accident means going with the currents that flow where you are going. Sometimes that means paying your dues, either literally, by joining organizations, or figuratively, by learning the ropes and jumping through the hoops related to your chosen path. When I chose coaching, I chose to get over myself and do whatever it took to become affiliated, certified, and legitimized in my chosen profession.

The day I realized I was a coach I joined the International Coach Federation (ICF), the professional organization that is responsible for coach training accreditation and coach certification. I kept an eye on the emerging training organizations, and in 1998 I enrolled in The Academy for Coach Training.

I thought I was a darn good coach before I went to The Academy (blush), and when I completed their program I was twice as effective and worked half as hard. I tell you this because I had been arrogant enough to think they wouldn't have much to teach me. (double blush).

I kept paying dues. In 2001, I completed the Newfield Network's Graduate Coach Training Program. I went on to study Embodied Intelligence in a seven-month program led by Charlie Badenhop and Cindy Franklin.* Since then I have invested thousands of dollars a year in professional development, including studying with Amy and Arnie Mindell† and completing The School for The Work of Byron Katie‡.

As to jumping through hoops, in 2001, I earned my Professional Certified Coach credential (PCC), and two years later I became a Master Certified Coach. I volunteered at the local and national levels of ICF, and I spoke at five ICF international conferences and a couple of regional ones.

I am blowing my own horn here to show you that my success was not instantaneous, magical, or inexpensive in terms of time, energy, or money. I did it a bit at a time, reinvested most of my earnings in professional development for the first five years that I was in business, and lived very modestly (and happily). That may not have impressed anyone else, but it impressed the heck out of me.

Doing What Comes Naturally

Line of least resistance, lead me on. ~Jesse Winchester

The Internet was exploding onto the scene at the same time that coaching started to develop as a separate profession. I loved exploring the ins and outs of every bit of software I could get my hands on, and I downloaded free software that enabled me to build my first Web site. I loved to write, so I wrote, and I posted

---

* www.seishindo.org

† www.aa-mindell.net

‡ www.thework.com.

my musings on various online bulletin boards. In short order I was hosting bulletin boards at some of the early portal sites, such as womenconnect.com and what is now findlaw.com

Because I didn't start out chasing business and I wasn't trying to coach more people than I had bandwidth for, I was able to be really present to the clients I had. This allowed me to be confident and enthusiastic when I talked about my work, especially when I did it in writing.

I did what came naturally, and I applied it as best I could to the needs of my business. I marketed myself online because I was more comfortable writing about what I was thinking and learning than I was giving elevator speeches at networking breakfasts. (I did try a couple of these. They practically gave me hives.) I realized that I did not know enough about what coaching was to talk about it in general, so I stuck to talking about what intrigued and challenged me, hoping to appeal to people who cared about the same sorts of things.

The point is that I used the materials at hand, including my natural talents and inclinations, to grow a business that really and truly fit me like a glove. From time to time, my ego would get involved and push for more fame, more money, or more action. I'd spin my wheels for a few days or weeks, get worn out and discouraged, and eventually remember that everything good that had happened so far had come from paying attention to what was right in front of me and hanging a left if I hit a wall.

I was learning to take care of my business by taking it a bit at a time. Acknowledging that you're in business can be overwhelming, even if you are familiar with the territory. If, like me, you'd never really thought of yourself as a business owner, it's like waking up in a foreign land. Not only do you not know where you are, you don't even know the language. If we try to move too fast, we're likely to decide that we don't like the country at all.

No Ducks in a Row

In retrospect, cooperating with accident looks pretty seamless. At the time, it looked and felt chaotic. In 1996 there was no way to know if the International Coach Federation (ICF) was going to survive, let alone play a major role in certifying coaches. There was no way to know if having a Website would be good for business or not.

I joined ICF and I became active online because these seemed like obvious (not "right") next steps. I did a lot of other things, like moderating online communities, which  proved to be dead ends. My point is that there was no way I could know what the "right" decision would be. More importantly, there was no need for me to know. I kept the goal in mind and took one step at a time toward it. If a step took me in the wrong direction, I stopped walking and turned around.

The early years of being in business are years of discovery. We can't possibly know what is ahead. We can, however, keep our eyes and ears and hearts open. We can pay attention to what works and what doesn't, regarding both as equally valuable teachers.

If we approach a new business the way an artist might approach a fresh canvas, we may discover that being in business is one of the best things that could have happened to us. Good things really do happen by accident. Time and again the things we could not have predicted (and may have struggled to avert) prove to be great blessings.

Chapter 3
The Art of Falling

My trusty dictionary defines entrepreneur as "a person who organizes and operates a business or businesses, taking on greater than normal financial risks in order to do so." When you decide to work for yourself—to generate your own paycheck, you become an entrepreneur. Not a hobbyist, not a volunteer, but an entrepreneur. Yikes! Who knew?

Accidents and the Art of Falling

Accidents are things that happen by chance, unintentionally or unexpectedly. The Latin roots of accident mean "to fall toward." As Accidental Entrepreneurs, we have fallen toward business. That's not a bad thing, but it can be confusing, especially when we don't realize what's going on.

In karate, falling is an art. We can make an art of falling into our businesses, as well. We can learn not just to survive falling, but to participate in it so that we land in one piece, safe and ready to do it again. Of course, this takes practice.

In the movie, *The Karate Kid*, Mr. Miyagi trains Daniel by having him wax cars, paint a fence, sand a wooden floor. In time he realizes that by performing these tedious and seemingly trivial tasks, he has mastered three of the most important Karate moves and, more importantly, he has learned that "the secret to karate lies in the mind and the heart, not in the hands."

The secret to successful self-employment also lies in the mind and heart. We become skilful entrepreneurs when we bring mindfulness to our day-to-day challenges, practicing a few fundamental "moves" as we respond to what life brings us. In this manner, "falling toward" business becomes art.

A Simple Path

We marvel at the ability of a master martial artist to fend off multiple opponents furiously attacking from different directions at the same time. How many moves must he have memorized? How can he keep track of everything that is happening in the midst of the melee when we, safe in the audience, can hardly follow what is going on?

From the outside, it seems that achieving such mastery must be incredibly complicated. But complicated is precisely what it is *not*. The path to mastery is a path of great simplicity.

Wild Birds

In 1987, a scientist named Craig Reynolds wrote a computer program (called Boids) that modeled the flocking behavior of wild birds.

"Each boid followed three simple rules of behavior:

It tried to maintain a minimum distance from other objects in the environment, including other boids.

It tried to match velocities with boids in its neighborhood.

It tried to move toward the perceived center of mass of boids in its neighborhood.

What was striking about these rules was that none of them said, 'Form a flock.' Quite the opposite: the rules were entirely local, referring only to what an individual boid could see and do in its own vicinity."*

---

* From Complexity - *The Emerging Science at the Edge of Order and Chaos* by M. Mitchell Waldrop.

The Way of the Accidental Entrepreneur also consists of three simple instructions:

1. **Question stressful thoughts.**
2. **Be Yourself.**
3. **Keep the channel open.**

These instructions, applied to what you (like the boids) can see and do in your own vicinity, combine to enable you to succeed at the complex tasks of growing a business that fits just-right. With these instructions, you can lead yourself to real material wellbeing, peace of mind, and the knowledge that you are serving something larger than your own self-interests with your business.

Is This Business?

The Three Instructions aren't the standard fare of MBA programs. But if you wanted an MBA, you'd be getting one instead of reading this book.

The truth is that doing business is not all that hard. Look at some of the people who excel at it, if you want proof. If you can add, subtract, and multiply, you can handle the financial side. If you can make yourself understood in your native tongue, you have sufficient communication ability.

It's not the systems and structures of business that can be so off-putting, it's the culture, at least the culture we usually associate with business success. The etiquette, dress code, and secret handshakes can seem stuffy, unfeeling, and self-seeking. The books, magazines, and articles seem to be written in a different language. Market forces. Target audiences. Campaigns. Is this making a living or making war?

Culture Shock

It's ironic that the Accidental Entrepreneur, who by and large values cultural diversity, should often have such an allergic reaction to the culture of business. This reaction creates a culture gap that, real or imagined, has very real consequences.

Culture gaps breed fear and mistrust. If you're suffering from a culture gap with the business world, the best business education in the world won't teach you how to grow a business that fits you just-right. For that, you'd need a universal translator, a way to learn from the world of business—a way that fits you. That's what our Three Instructions are intended to be.

Let's take a brief look at the instructions as they relate to this issue of a culture gap with business.

Question Stressful Thoughts

When our Reality doesn't jibe with the story or mythology we've thought of as defining business success, an Accidental Entrepreneur may see business as a club she doesn't belong to—perhaps one she doesn't even really want to join, or couldn't get into if she tried. This kind of outsider identity can be supported by an array of stressful thoughts.

Thoughts like:

I just want to do good work. Why should I have to sell myself?
It's hard to make a living in (enter the field of your choice).
Customers won't tolerate mistakes.
People don't like to be sold to.
My friends will be hurt if I tell them not to drop by during the day.
My spouse always told me I didn't have what it takes to go it alone.
They won't pay me.

Thoughts like these are like excess baggage on a cross-country hike. Conventional success guides would have you turn them into affirmations or pulverize them with the mallet of positive thinking. But affirmations and positive thinking don't work on core beliefs, have you noticed? When we apply them to our stressful thoughts about business, we feel phony, silly, or—if we buy into the notion that we should be able to change our thoughts—like spiritual dunces. What's more, affirmations and positive thinking keep us from the pearl in the oyster, the realization or insight that awaits us when we question stressful thoughts.

It's likely that you've worked your way out of a number of dead-end situations by questioning your thoughts, though you may not have defined it that way. Perhaps you caught yourself in mid-rant about one thing or another and something in the tone of your own voice pulled you up short. If the need to be right didn't have you by the throat, maybe you noticed that you were making a mountain out of a molehill. Maybe you realized that there was another way to understand the situation that was kinder and more accurate.

The Work of Byron Katie®

In 2002, two readers of my newsletter told me I needed to check out The Work of Byron Katie. (When we connect with the just-right audience, the help never stops.) I listened to the audiotapes of her first book, *Loving What Is,* and I was hooked. Here was a clear, simple way to do what I'd always done by stumbling and struggling and usually only after a lot of pain: question stressful thoughts.

The Work consists of identifying a stressful thought, asking four questions, and turning the thought around. We'll go into the process in much more depth later. For now, here are the questions.

1. **Is it true?**
2. **Can you absolutely know that it's true?**
3. **How do you react when you think that thought? What happens?**
4. **Who would you be without the thought?**

After answering the four questions, we look for opposites of the stressful thought. *They won't pay me* turns around to *They will pay me.* Another turnaround for the same thought is *I won't pay me.* A third is *I won't pay them.* We go inside and sit with each turnaround, checking to see if it could be as true or truer than the original thought.

When we bring a stressful thought to The Work, often we find that the thought lets go of us—we don't have to struggle to let go of it—as we realize it actually isn't true for us. The way forward opens up from there.

Be Yourself

At the root of culture shock is the fear that we don't belong and won't ever fit in. In response, we adopt a variety of strategies, all of which involve trying to be something we are not.

We can deny that we are afraid and be defiant or disrespectful of the cultural norms of business. We can pretend that we understand what we don't, which makes it hard to learn and easy to look ridiculous. We can be over-polite, walking on eggshells or fawning over our customers.

Not only are these poses usually unsustainable, they conceal the value we legitimately have to offer. Each of us has a certain something that delights our just-right customers. It is this something that distinguishes our work from the work of someone else. (Oddly enough, as you'll see in the following example, we may try to hide what makes us special.) Walking the Way of the Accidental Entrepreneur requires us to be ourselves in the service of others and of our own businesses.

Example: Mom + Daughter = Good Business

Maggie and Anne make stained glass windows. They came to one of my workshops wanting to learn how to promote their work. During the day, I asked participants to answer a number of questions, including what they most feared their prospective clients or customers would find out about them and their work.

Maggie and Anne confessed that they were afraid that they wouldn't be taken seriously if people found out that they were a self-taught mother and daughter team that worked out of Maggie's garage. But everyone in the room that day thought their story was interesting—everyone, that is, except Maggie and Anne.

I challenged them to include their relationship and background in their brochures and conversations with prospective buyers. When they stopped trying to cover up the truth, their enthusiasm for stained glass was obvious. A few months after they started mentioning their relationship in press releases, a local newspaper ran a feature story about them and their work. The fact that they were a mom and daughter was the "hook" for the story. It's what made them unique.

Exercise: What Are You Hiding?

What secrets are you keeping from your prospective clients and customers? Complete the following sentence stem to find out. Repeat it as many times as necessary to get all your secrets down on paper.

People wouldn't hire me if they knew _____

Secrecy Versus Privacy

It's important to distinguish between keeping secrets and respecting your privacy. You don't owe anyone an emotional strip tease. It isn't kind to them (or to you) to share every personal detail. On the other hand, a business that fits just-right is one in which you can be authentic. Look at what you've been hiding and ask yourself if some of the things that embarrass you might be valuable and even charming to the right clients and customers.

It's All Connected

How do you find out what you have to offer through being yourself? One way is to use The Work to question thoughts that would have you believe who you are is not okay or that no one wants what you have to offer. As you can see already, our three simple instructions are inter-related. The Way of the Accidental Entrepreneur is organic, not linear. We follow each instruction when it can help, and often we will find that we are following all three more or less at the same time.

Another way to Be Yourself is to practice awareness. Are you in your body? Are you in the present? Is your attention on your business (as in "mind your own beeswax") or someone else's? Noticing what is happening here and now brings us back to our authentic selves, the only place from which we can grow our authentic businesses.

Keep the Channel Open

Questioning stressful thoughts frees you to apply your skills and intelligence to growing a business. Being yourself ensures that the business you grow is one that fits just-right. Keeping the channel open is how you maintain connection with the Source of it all

Whether you are a painter or a surgeon, your best work happens when you allow some greater intelligence to work through you. Aligning yourself with the Source of that intelligence is essential to your wellbeing, to the growth of your business, and to the value you deliver through your work.

You and your business are not the Source of value, but the conduit or channel through which value flows to your clients and customers. Take care of the conduit, and the Source will take care of the rest.

Keeping the channel open requires us to be ourselves; it also makes it safe for us to do so. When we contort ourselves in an effort to be "businesslike," the conduit gets twisted, blocking the flow of grace, insight and courage. When we accept ourselves and the world around us even when we don't know exactly how it will all work out, we wake up to the support that is always present. That culture gap seems to shrink before our eyes as soon as we shift our attention to our own Source.

Fall with Your Eyes Open

If the culture gap is going to shrink before our eyes, we need to have our eyes open. Keeping your eyes open is a sort of master key to success as an Accidental Entrepreneur. Each of the

Three Instructions helps us open our eyes at critical points along the path.

When assumptions or fears blind you to what is just-right, Questioning Stressful Thoughts will open your eyes to what is perfect in this moment. When preoccupation with how you think you should be obscures the value of what you have to offer, Being Yourself will turn the light back on. And when you feel lost and unable to see the way ahead, remembering to Keep the Channel Open will show you the next indicated step.

Chapter 4

How to Use this Book

re you wondering why a chapter called "How to Use this Book" isn't at the beginning? Beginnings can be problematic for the Accidental Entrepreneur. Where does your life end and your business begin? When did being who you are turn into working for yourself? In a very real sense, The Way of the Accidental Entrepreneur is a way without a beginning or end. We begin where we are.

I'm a coach, but I didn't always have coaches to help me with my business. For a long time I simply couldn't afford one. Instead, I coached myself using the Three Instructions you've just read about. This book is the sum of my experience plus tips for walking the same path.

To get the most out of it, use this book like a personal coach. Like a coach, it will ask you a lot of questions. Like a coach, it will encourage you as you look for your own answers. And like a coach, it will challenge you to reach beyond your current ways of knowing and being.

Establish a Coaching Relationship

The essence of coaching is the relationship between coach and client. Unlike friends, colleagues, employees, or family members, the coach is a neutral party, albeit one with a profound commitment to the wellbeing and growth of the client. This neutrality combined with commitment makes it possible for the client to do deep work safely and creatively.

To be your own coach you will need to approximate both the compassionate neutrality and the commitment of a coach. That can be quite a trick, and I know you are up to it. You probably already bring both neutrality and commitment to other relationships and situations. Now I ask you to make a conscious choice to adopt that way of being when you work on your business.

This means being both kind and rigorous as you apply the Three Instructions as needed to heal wounds, release biases, perceive possibilities, gather strength, make choices, and evaluate results. Of course, this is an ideal. There will be times when you are harsh with yourself and times when you are self-indulgent; (sue you for being human). When you notice, begin again. The path is always under your feet.

Basic Framework for a Coaching Session

A basic framework for self-coaching can be summed up with a few questions. Whatever aspect of your business you are working on, you can use this framework to focus your work.

What did I do?

What do I know about the topic?

What actions have I taken? (Not acting is an action!)

Which of the Three Instructions did I follow? (if applicable)

What happened?

What did that feel like?

Where did it leave me?

What questions were answered?

What new questions showed up?

What will I do now?

What result do I want?

What's in the way?

What resources do I have?
Which of the Three Instructions will I follow now?

These questions presuppose that you come to the session with a topic. The topic may be narrow (work on your business card) or broad (fear of marketing). In either case, the more specific you are, the easier it will be to make measurable progress.

Document Your Work

Document your self-coaching in writing. There are many reasons for doing this; here are three. First, when you record your process in writing you involve your senses of touch, vision, and hearing. This makes your experience more vivid and more memorable.

Secondly, recording your process gives you incontrovertible evidence that you are walking your talk. When self-doubt and self-criticism rise up, you can demonstrate your commitment and follow through.

Thirdly, keeping a record will help you mark milestones and celebrate successes. When you simply take one step after another, it is easy to get lost in the daily details of the journey. The path can feel tedious and never-ending. Paradoxically, this takes you out of the present moment by inviting a comparison with some more desirable future or destination.

Make documentation as simple as possible so that it doesn't become a barrier. You can use the example below as a model. A spiral notebook is a great way to keep track of your notes. If you are computer-savvy and prefer to work digitally, keep your notes on your computer. The point is to anchor your experience of working on your business in writing on a regular basis. It's better to make a few brief notes during each session than to describe some sessions in excruciating detail and skip over others.

Self-Coaching Example: Naming the Business

Nancy, a massage therapist, needs a name for her business. She's read a couple of magazine articles about naming businesses as well as a book about branding. They all made sense when she was reading them, but they contradict each other, and now she is confused. Here's an example of how Nancy used self-coaching to get unstuck.

Topic: Naming my business.

What did I do?

I read articles and a book about branding. I've talked to some other bodyworkers. I've played with some names.

What happened?

The articles and book made sense when I was reading them, but they contradict each other. Other bodyworkers were supportive, but not very informative. The ones who have full practices don't know if their business names mattered, and the ones who need clients are all over the place.

What will I do now?

Well, I'm doing this coaching session, but I guess I need to look at what I want out of it. I want to name the business so that I can get my business cards made up and get a business phone.

What's in the way?

I'm afraid of doing it wrong. If I don't choose a good name, it could keep me from getting clients.

What resources do I have?

I have my study group. I can ask them to help me get past this fear.

Which of the Three Instructions will I follow now?

I can use The Work to question my stressful thought about needing to get this right. I can lighten up and remember that a name that fits my personality and attitude toward my work will feel good to me and that will be good for customers. I can take a break from this and go for a walk.

You Can Do This

It's natural to think that something is wrong when we fall, even if we're in a karate class. When we fall, an ancient survival reflex floods our systems with adrenaline and other neuro-chemicals that scream, "Emergency!" Our bodies are readied to fight, freeze, or flee. When we're in real trouble, this is terrific. When we're not, it's not.

When fear is chronic, the survival reflex becomes a self-fulfilling prophecy. For example, if we fear that clients won't want to pay the fee we need to charge to make a good living, we bring that fear to every conversation about price. We equivocate (freeze), avoid naming our price (flee), or are defensive (fight). None of these conversational styles are likely to put our prospective clients at ease, and usually they walk away without hiring us. Our fear has produced the result we feared and proven that we were right to be afraid.

Often, we are at least marginally aware of how being afraid creates the results we fear. Unfortunately, we may turn that self-awareness against ourselves, beating ourselves up for not successfully applying any one of the umpteen approaches to setting and naming fees that we may have read about. After a while, we might begin to believe that we are handicapped when it comes to business by virtue of who we are and what we care about. But that simply isn't true—the turn-around is truer: in fact, our strength is who we are and what we care about.

Our handicap, if we have one, is in our (often unconscious) belief that falling—experiencing overwhelm, confusion, and or disorientation—means that we are in real trouble. We mistakenly assume that, at best, success will exact too high a price and leave too many scars.

In other words, if our identities are tied to not being good at business, we have a case of mistaken identity. But when we realize that falling is a natural part of doing business and simply follow the Three Instructions that enable us to turn business into art, everything changes.

Just-Right

Remember the story of Goldilocks, the little girl who went for a walk in the woods and discovered a cottage, whereupon she tried the porridge, chairs, and beds until she found what suited her just-right.

Like many good-hearted people who work for themselves, you may believe success requires you to settle for a business that doesn't quite suit you. What's more, your idea of what that business would be like is probably mixed up with a hodge-podge of myth, prejudice, and fear. Some characteristics of your imagined business feel inauthentic and dishonest—too hot! Others are too good to be true (build it and they will come)—too cold!

What Makes a Business Fit Just Right?

If you've been working for yourself for a while, you can answer that question simply by looking at what feels wrong. If you feel icky about marketing, a just right business is one in which marketing will feel good.

Similarly, if you are thinking about going out on your own, your worries will tell you what makes a business fit just right. If you are worried about what to charge for your services, for example, you know that a business that feels just right is one where you and your just-right clients are both satisfied with your fees.

If Goldilocks Can Do It, So Can You

If Goldilocks can steal into the home of the three bears, find a bowl of porridge, a chair, and a bed that are just right for her, and get out alive (at least in some versions of the tale), you can attain prosperity, peace, and fulfillment from the world of business.

A Way of Life

It's an old gag. A guy walks into an office and asks for the boss. The clerk, who walks with an exaggerated limp, says, "Walk this way." The guy follows the clerk, faithfully imitating his limp.

I know. Dumb joke. But once I started musing on the meaning of "way," I couldn't get it out of my head. The last thing I had intended was to write a "do it this way" book. But, in spite of myself, I started to wonder: what if this book is about a way of walking rather than the path to be walked?

Today this seems like another BFO (blinding flash of the obvious). The truth is, I don't know your path. Shoot, most days I don't know mine. What I do know is a way of walking that works for me. Since you're reading this, I believe it is a way that will work for you, too.

As Accidental Entrepreneurs, we don't want to succeed at business and fail at life. By following the Three Instructions as you meet the day-to-day challenges of growing your business, you will enrich your personal life as well. The Way of the Accidental Entrepreneur is a way of life before it is a way of making a living.

Chapter 5
Question Stressful Thoughts

At first glance, questioning stressful thoughts may seem like an odd tool for building a business. In my experience, it is actually the single most useful tool available to the Accidental Entrepreneur. But if you believe you need to "suck it up" and "stick it out" in order to succeed, you may wonder what good it will do to question the inevitable.

Here's the key: you won't be questioning *Reality*, but rather, your *thoughts* about Reality. When our thoughts agree with Reality, we experience peace. When our thoughts argue with Reality, we experience stress.

The purpose of questioning stressful thoughts is to reconcile with Reality. Reality is always kinder than the thought that argues with it. The Reality that you have fewer clients than a peer does not cause stress. Stress occurs when you believe the thought that there is something wrong with the number you have.

Questioning stressful thoughts frees up our creativity. As soon as we stop arguing with the way things are, we are free to act in behalf of what we want. Any time we argue with Reality we are investing our precious life energy in a losing game. If you lose a client, thinking that you shouldn't have won't bring her back.

There are a number of ways to question stressful thoughts. You may have learned one or more of them, and you may realize as you read this section that whenever you have gotten free from a resentment or fear you did it by questioning a stressful thought, even if you did not think of it that way at the time.

30

The Work of Byron Katie®

Of all the methods of inquiry I've studied, The Work of Byron Katie is the simplest, most elegant, and most kind.

The Work originated when Katie (as she is known) woke up on the floor of a women's treatment center to see a cockroach crawling over her bare foot. Not an altogether auspicious beginning! But for Katie, who had spent the previous ten years imprisoned by depression, agoraphobia, eating disorders, and addictions, it was the moment of awakening. In that instant, she realized that her desperate state was not caused by the world around her, but by her beliefs about it.

"Katie saw that when she believed that something should be different than it is ('My husband should love me more,' 'My children should appreciate me') she suffered, and that when she *didn't* believe these thoughts, she felt peace. She realized that what had been causing her depression was not the world around her, but the beliefs she had about the world around her. In a flash of insight, Katie saw that our attempt to find happiness was backward — instead of hopelessly trying to change the world to match our thoughts about how it 'should' be, we can question these thoughts and, by meeting Reality as it is, experience unimaginable freedom and joy."*

Four Questions and Turnarounds

The Work entails writing down a stressful or painful thought, asking four questions, and then turning the original thought around to see if the turnaround is as true or truer than the original thought. It's that simple. Let's look at an example.

---

* From *Loving What Is*, by Byron Kathleen Mitchell. *Loving What Is* is the basic text for The Work. It is essential reading for the Accidental Entrepreneur.

Example: They Don't Respect My Work

Marian submitted a proposal to deliver a presentation at a conference. She has just received the letter saying that hers was not among the proposals selected. One of her stressful thoughts is, "They don't respect my work." Here is her written inquiry.

They don't respect my work.

Is it true? *Yes.*

Can I absolutely know that it is true? *No.*

How do I react when I believe that thought? *I feel awful. My temples get tight and my chest hurts. I imagine the committee members making fun of my proposal or rolling their eyes while they discuss it. I worry that I will never receive the recognition I need to succeed. I beat myself up for not starting to write my proposal earlier. I snap at my husband when he asks about my day.*

Who would I be without the thought? *Relaxed. I'd be looking forward to the conference. I might even be relieved that I don't have to prepare a presentation.*

How to Do the Turnarounds

Turnarounds are reversals of the stressful thought we brought to inquiry. To find the turnarounds, write down the thought you questioned. Restate it in one or all of the following ways:

Turnaround to the opposite.
Turnaround to the other.
Turnaround to the self.

When you find a turnaround, go inside and check to see if it is as true or truer than the original thought. Keep it simple! This is not a debate or a contest. You're not trying to disprove your original thought, you are simply inviting an exploration of its other sides. Just go in and wait until you see what's so for you. If you find that the turnaround is as true or truer, see if you can find three concrete, specific examples of that from your own experience.

Turnaround to the Opposite

There can be two ways to turn a thought around to the opposite: changing a negative statement to positive or vice versa, and using words that have the opposite meaning of key words in the original thought. Here's how Marian found her turnarounds (for the thought, "They don't respect my work").

Reverse positive/negative: *They do respect my work.*

Reverse meaning: *They admire my work.*

Turnaround to the Other

When we judge others for something they did to us, we can often turn the statement around by putting ourselves in their place and vice versa. For example, *I don't respect their work.*

Turnaround to the Self

Finally, we can turn the statement around by putting ourselves in both places. For example, *I don't respect my work.*

Is the Turnaround as True or Truer?

Our work with turnarounds is not complete until we can find examples of how they are as true or truer (if we find they are, for us). Here are the examples Marian found for her turnarounds.

They do respect my work. *This is truer. They invited me to submit a proposal. They thanked me for submitting the proposal. They considered the proposal.*

They admire my work. *This is truer. They invited me to submit this year. They asked me to submit again next year. Mary told me that the committee loved my proposal but that they did not have room for another advanced session.*

I don't respect their work. *This is truer. I don't respect their work when I look for ulterior motives to explain their selections. I don't respect their work when I make the proposal process into a* *popularity contest. I don't respect their work when I think I could do a better job.*

I don't respect my work. This is truer. I don't respect my work when I imagine them judging it negatively. I don't respect my work when I obsess about whether or not they respect it. I don't respect my work when I value it only if it receives outside acknowledgement.

Underlying Beliefs

Your answers to question three, "What happens? How do I react when I believe that thought?" often reveal underlying stressful beliefs. For example, Marian found these underlying beliefs in her answer to question three.

I need recognition to succeed.
I should have started my proposal earlier.

She wrote these beliefs in her journal so she could question them in turn.

Spinning

Suppose that Marian stopped in the middle of her inquiry to explore one of her underlying beliefs. When we jump from thought to thought instead of sitting with the original thought until we have finished Inquiry, we end up going in circles. This is called spinning.

This is one reason for doing The Work on paper instead of in your head.

Tips for Doing The Work on Your Own

You can do The Work alone or with a partner. If you are working alone, write out the questions and answers. It's important to do The Work in writing because our minds don't hold still while we examine a thought. Writing the thought down allows us to stay in the process of inquiry until we are complete.

You can ask anyone who can read the four questions to be your partner. You can also experience skilled facilitation by using the free Hotline staffed by volunteers who have completed the nine-day School for The Work. *

Keep It Simple

The Work is four questions and turnarounds, no more, no less. You can inquire into stressful beliefs in other ways, but the way to do The Work is to ask the questions, wait for the answers, and explore the turnarounds. Making it more complicated won't help, and it can get in the way of the realizations you seek.

Judge Others

Beginners in The Work are encouraged to judge others instead of themselves. That can be surprising, even disconcerting. Aren't we supposed to love our neighbor?

Well, yes, and what's the Reality?

Customers are demanding. Clients are late for appointments. A peer starts using the quote you've been using in your email signature in hers. As an Accidental Entrepreneur, you have oodles of opportunities to be upset, angry, worried, or fearful in reaction to what others do or don't do.

You can spend your days hating yourself for being judgmental, or you can do The Work and turn those judgments into freedom and clarity about your next step.

Can You Do The Work on Yourself?

Sometimes it may seem that all your stressful thoughts are about you. Can you take thoughts like these to The Work? Yes, and The Work won't "work" if we go in with a motive. When we take self-judgments to The Work, our desire for relief, or an insight that will get us unstuck, or justification, will affect the answers we find.

Even subconscious motives influence the way we answer the four questions. They create biases that keep us from being truly

---

* Visit www.institioteforthework.com and look for the Hotline.

open to the turnarounds. We may end up frustrated and feeling abandoned when The Work doesn't solve our problem.

Unless you are quite experienced in The Work, I suggest that you project your judgments outward. If you feel you must question a self-judgment, ask a friend to facilitate you or call The Hotline.* An experienced facilitator can help you steer clear of your motives.

How to Project Self-Judgments Outward

There are several ways to convert a self-judgment into a judgment projected outward. If your judgment is about the consequences of an action or way of being, just substitute the category of people who share that action or way of being for yourself. "If I don't stop procrastinating, I'll never finish this book," becomes "Writers who procrastinate don't finish their books."

If your judgment is about a trait you should or shouldn't have, add the word "because" to your statement, list the reasons, then judge them. For example, working with the belief, "I should be more assertive," you might come up with the following reasons.

I should be more assertive because:
People will take advantage of me if I am not.
People should stand up for themselves.
People who don't assert themselves can't succeed in business.
People who aren't assertive have low self-esteem.

---

* The free hotline is staffed by volunteers who have completed the nine-day School for The Work. Details at www.thework.com.

Example: Projecting Self-Judgments Outward

I found many opportunities to do The Work while writing this book. Sometimes I questioned my thoughts about me. Other times I found ways to project my thoughts outward.

For example, I had the thought that I was procrastinating. When I questioned that, I found myself going in circles (spinning) because I had a motive: I wanted to stop procrastinating or, if I didn't stop, to justify it so I could feel good about it. Needless to say, this got in the way of finding my honest answers to the four questions.

In order to get past this, I asked myself what it was about procrastinating that was a problem. Here are some of the thoughts I came up with:

Writers who procrastinate fail to finish their books.
Writers who procrastinate are dishonest.
Writers who procrastinate get in trouble with their readers.

When I did The Work on my judgments about writers in general I found it easier to answer the questions without bias.

Be Petty

Sometimes the most amazing shifts can arise from questioning the pettiest thoughts. People shouldn't cut in front of me in traffic. The clerk at the post office should be more efficient. People should use better subject lines in their emails.

What If My Stressful Thought Is True?

Sometimes you may feel stress about something that is demonstrably true. What's going on here?

Reality is not stressful. If a true statement appears to be causing your stress, it is not the Reality of it but your thoughts about that Reality that are the problem.

Let's say that your office rent is $500, and the Reality is that you have $200 in your checking account. It's not the difference between what you have and what you owe that produces stress, it's your thoughts about that difference. The fact, "There's not enough money in the bank for this month's rent," is not, in itself, stressful.

"There's not enough money in the bank for this month's rent, *and it means that I am a failure*" is stressful. When you feel stress about something that is factual, add the phrase "it means that" to the true statement. Make a list, and question each item.

Cultivate "I Don't Know" Mind

Notice the tendency to answer the four questions from "I know" mind. If the answers you have already were helpful, you wouldn't be experiencing stress. Instead, when you ask the questions, go inside to where you don't already know the answers. Listen with open curiosity as if you were sitting with a friend over a cup of tea, not knowing yet where the conversation might go.

In this way, the answers will rise to meet the question. You won't have to figure them out. And, as your answers arise, the beliefs that were causing stress undo themselves. You don't have to chase them away, let go of them, or practice affirmations. Everything required for peace will happen of its own accord so long as you are present and seeking the truth.

Thoughts Are Not the Enemy

The point of The Work is not to get rid of your thoughts. That's not going to happen, and it is not necessary. For one thing, your thoughts are not the cause of the stress you experience. Your stress is the result of believing a thought that argues with Reality.

The more you do The Work, the freer you become. As you gain experience in The Work, you may find that you actually look forward to noticing your stressful thoughts.

Skipping Ahead to the Turnarounds

After a while, you may think you can skip the four questions and go straight to the turnarounds. After all, that's where the action is, right?

Wrong. The Work is not about reversing your thoughts or proving them wrong. It's not about replacing a "bad" thought with a "better" one. It's about ending the war with yourself, the war that heats up whenever you argue with Reality.

Asking and answering the four questions prepares the mind to discover the truth in the turnarounds without attacking itself. Going to the turnarounds without asking the four questions is like doing surgery with a blunt knife and no anesthetic.

Turning The Work into a Concept

When we generalize our experience in The Work, we are constructing new concepts. That's okay, but eventually those concepts are likely to conflict with Reality, and then we may feel that The Work has failed us.

Case Study: When The Work Doesn't Work

Angie, a physical therapist, did The Work with her coach about a client who did not do his at-home routine. Kate felt the routine was essential to recovery, and she worried that the client would blame her if he didn't get better.

Angie questioned the thought, "He will blame me if he doesn't get better," and found the turnaround, "I will blame me if he doesn't get better." As she sat with that, she realized that she did not feel good about continuing to treat her client unless he agreed to do his at-home routine.

Angie told the client that she didn't feel right about continuing unless he agreed to do his practices. He thanked her for being so frank, agreed to do his at-home routine, and got better rapidly.

A few months later, Angie showed up for a coaching session in tears because she had lost three clients. Her coach offered to facilitate her in The Work. "The Work doesn't work," Angie complained. "I lost those clients because I told them that they had to do their homework or I wouldn't continue treating them."

Exploring the situation with her coach, Angie realized that she had generalized her earlier Work into the concept, "As long as I am honest with my clients, they will do what I want them to do." When this new belief conflicted with Reality, Angie thought that The Work had failed her.

Will The Work Make You Passive?

Sometimes newcomers to The Work are afraid it will make them passive, even apathetic. They worry that such radical acceptance could make them insensitive to the suffering of others. What if you feel stress because you know a child is suffering from an abusive parent? Does questioning the thought mean condoning abuse?

The Work is about *realizing* truth, not avoiding it. The idea that The Work might make us passive or apathetic has its roots in the belief that we need stress to motivate us to respond to pain. But do you need to be motivated to soothe a crying child? Sing a favorite song? Pick up a cup to take a drink?

As Katie says, The Work frees the mind to love, and love feeds the hungry child. When we are not attached to painful thoughts, we are free to serve others in any way that presents itself.

Let's Do The Work

You've been reading a lot about how to do The Work, and you probably have some questions. Instead of trying to anticipate and answer those questions, I invite you to do The Work right now.

You will need a pen, paper, and a stressful thought to question. If one doesn't immediately come to mind, you can choose one from the following list or use the Judge Your Neighbor worksheet*.

---

* There is a total of six questions on the worksheet, only the first four appear here. Download a free Judge Your Neighbor worksheets from the resource section at www.thework.com to see all six questions, including special instructions for turning around your answer to question six.

Stressful Thoughts About Working for Yourself

She doesn't respect my work.

Selling is manipulative.

S/he won't pay me because I made a mistake.

My family won't leave me alone during work hours.

The Judge Your Neighbor Worksheet

If none of those thoughts rings true, complete a Judge Your Neighbor worksheet. Answer each question in short, simple sentences. Be petty and childish. This is an opportunity for all those thoughts we try to push away to express themselves without hurting anyone.

1. Who angers, disappoints, or confuses you, and why? What is it about them that you don't like?
2. How do you want them to change? What do you want them to do?
3. What is it that they should or shouldn't do, be, think or feel? What advice could you offer?
4. Do you need anything from them? What do they need to do in order for you to be happy?

Example: Adam Judges His Ex-partner Henry

1. Who angers, disappoints, or confuses you, and why? What is it about them that you don't like?

   I'm angry at Henry for backing out of our business partnership. I hate that he led me on.

2. How do you want them to change? What do you want them to do?

   I want Henry to stop pretending to support me when he doesn't intend to follow through.

3. What is it that they should or shouldn't do, be, think or feel? What advice could you offer?

   Henry shouldn't lead people on. He should be ashamed of himself.

4. **Do you need anything from them? What do they need to do in order for you to be happy?**

I need him to apologize. I need him to help me get my business off the ground.

Do The Work

Write your stressful thought on a clean page in your notebook. Then write out your answers to each of the four questions. You may find it helps to read a question, then close your eyes and turn your attention inward. Wait until the answer appears, then open your eyes and write your answer down. The four questions and cues for the turnarounds reappear below. You can also refer to the example beginning on page 32.

1. Is it true?
2. Can I absolutely know that it is true?
3. How do I react when I believe that thought? What happens?
4. Who would I be without this thought?

Turnarounds

Turn around to the opposite
Turn around to the other
Turn around to the self

Chapter 6

Be Yourself

The second Instruction, *Be Yourself*, can be easier said than done. However committed you may be to authenticity and integrity (and I know you are committed to both), you may find yourself making choices based on what you think others want rather than what is true for you.

Which Self Should You Be?

Another obstacle to being yourself is the notion that self is a static entity, a collection of invariable traits and preferences. There is a saying that expresses this: *A leopard can't change its spots.* It sounds incontrovertible, and it is utterly irrelevant to the human phenomenon of self.

Without waxing too philosophical about the nature of "self," we can say it has something to do with our experience of identity. And identity shifts with context. If that sounds bizarre, consider who you'd be, what identity you'd experience and express, in each of these situations:

Making your first speech in front of an audience.

Being informed that you owe $10,000 in back taxes.

Meeting the Dalai Lama.

I'm betting that the way you'd experience yourself shifts drastically as you imagine each of those events. In the case of making your first speech, you may have identified with being a beginner, a star, or an accident waiting to happen. When you imagined that you owed back taxes, you may have identified with being a victim of the system, an innocent citizen, or a cheat caught in the act. And when you imagined meeting the Dalai Lama, you may have identified with being a spiritual seeker, a cynic, or an academic. (And of course, there is any number of other possible identities.)

The point is that who we are changes with what we think about ourselves and whatever we are experiencing outside of ourselves. So how in the heck can you follow the instruction to Be Yourself, and what good would it do if you could?

Being and Growing

You know those maps you see on large campuses or at malls, the ones with the arrow marked, "You are here"? The arrow doesn't say "You are lost" or "You should be ashamed of yourself." Only "You are here."

If you aren't accustomed to doing business, you'll probably go through an awkward stage before getting comfortable. And the truth is that every business owner goes through not one but multiple awkward stages. That's the nature of growth.

But there's a difference between an awkward stage and a train wreck. It's awkward to step out of your comfort zone; it's a disaster to walk off a cliff.

Growing requires us to engage and express the self we experience *now* as fully as we can while remaining open to change. That is what Be Yourself means in The Way of the Accidental Entrepreneur.

How Can You Tell If You Are Being Yourself?

It's actually quite simple. When you are being yourself, your energy is going into whatever you are doing rather than into managing your image or fixing what's wrong with you.

When you follow this instruction, learning and growth will happen. As psychologist Carl Rogers observed, "When I experience and accept myself exactly as I am, I change."

Growth can't happen without acceptance and it can't be avoided when you are fully present.

How Does Being Yourself Help?

How does this instruction help you grow a business that fits just right?

In the first place, following this instruction gives dignity to your process. No matter how many mistakes you make, no matter how often you get lost along the way, if you are being yourself, you are present, which is right where you are supposed to be, and you are learning, which is an honorable endeavor.

Own Your Authority

While your self is always a work in progress, it is also the basis for owning your authority. You've done what you've done, been where you've been, and here you are. What you bring to each moment constitutes your authority.

Your authority is not defined by or in competition with anyone else's authority. Authority, in these sense I'm using it here, is authorship, writing the very next piece of your story out of awareness of what has gone before and what is happening now. It is about creating, not dictating. Authority is choice, not control.

As an Accidental Entrepreneur, it is essential that you own what you know. This authority, when it is based in guidance from Source, is your surest guide to a business that fits just-right.

What Are You Up to Today?

It's one thing to Be Yourself when you like the person you see in the mirror. It's another matter when you don't. What do you do when your evil twin takes charge?

I once attended a workshop with an artist who was teaching us to make retablos: painted tin shrines. Though I've forgotten her, I'll never forget how she described her morning routine.

When I get up the first thing I do is look in the mirror. I say to myself, "You are a liar and a thief, but that's not what I'm up to today."

Pre-occupied as I was at the time with patching up an ego battered by my experiments in being a bad girl, I was half-thrilled and half-horrified. I got the value of acknowledging one's faults, but I was naïve enough to think that my faults could be relegated to a permanent past.

Eventually I realized that my faults had not gone away. That's when I understood how potent it could be to acknowledge the liar and thief in the mirror while declaring an alternate intention for the day. We can acknowledge our vices and our moods without being at their mercy.

Moody Blues

The English word "mood" stems from the Indo-European root "med," meaning "measure." That's fitting, because the mood in which we do business establishes the measure of what is possible.

You can demonstrate this to yourself by imagining that a prospective client phones about an hour after you learn you've received a top award in your field. It's a great honor, and it comes with a cash prize of $5,000. How are you going to show up in the phone conversation?

Now imagine that a prospect phones when you are in the throes of a sustained funk. You've had a nagging cold all week. It's the first of the month and two of the credit charges for fees failed to go through. You wouldn't have answered the phone except you are waiting to hear back from your clients. How do you show up now?

Like a soundtrack, change the mood and you change the movie. But sometimes we don't want to change our moods. We cling to even painful moods when they prove our version of

Reality. If it is important to you to be right (who, me?), you may hang onto the mood of resentment, because letting it go is like saying being right doesn't matter.

But That's the Way I Feel

Feelings are not facts. When we confuse the way we feel with the way we are, our moods shut down the access to Source. When we are in the grip of a mood, we are closed to possibilities and stuck in an unsatisfactory present.

When a negative mood persists, look for the story that it legitimizes. Are you angry because you lost a client? It may be a fact that the client is gone, but facts are not problems, they are just facts.

Getting at the underlying story that makes a fact into a problem can be difficult. It's usually easier to see this in others than in ourselves. Here are some ways to get at the problem-creating story when it isn't immediately apparent.

Call a member of your support team and vent about what you are feeling. Tell them you don't want them to agree or disagree, but to listen for underlying beliefs.

Start a topic at Shaboom County by venting about the situation. Don't try to be mature or evolved, just let 'er rip. Be petty. Ask other members to tell you what underlying beliefs or stories show up for them.

Write a Judge Your Neighbor worksheet on the situation. See page 41 for an example.

The Myth of the Bright Path

There is a myth in our culture that the path to success should be bright. If discouragement or depression come calling, we simply need meditate more, take the right supplements, use the right affirmations, visualize white light, and things will be perfect.

Well, things *are* perfect, but sometimes perfection feels crummy. That presents a challenge that those of us who are self-employed feel keenly, especially if we think that perfection is supposed to feel and look great all the time.

What if success has less to do with image and more to do with substance? What if, for the accidental entrepreneur, success has more to do with the learner you are than the expert you have become?

Errors are the compost for success. Even with this understanding, you may wonder how to be with discouragement and even desperation without being defined by them. Here are some guidelines.

Begin by noticing and recording your dark experiences without judging, fixing, or resisting them. One way to practice the art of simply noticing is to observe and name the physical sensations that show up at a difficult time.

 Breathe. There is no situation that is improved by holding your breath. If it feels right, you might notice how effortlessly you are supported in the simple and involuntary act of breathing. (If you are as cranky as I sometimes am, it may not work to think a happy thought, so don't.)

Refrain from big decisions. It is usually possible to put off big decisions until we are feeling better. This is not procrastination, but waiting until you have sufficient information and perspective to decide.

Take small, necessary actions. Follow through as best you can with daily commitments and practices (exercise, rest, meditation). If you don't feel like walking for an hour, walk around the block.

Use the practices and rituals of your spiritual tradition to get the nourishment and support you need. Let yourself be imperfect in this so that you don't cut yourself off from Source at the moment you most need connection.

Hold yourself and your concerns gently and compassionately, asking for grace to heal, to see more clearly, to forgive yourself and others, to release the past, to discern next steps.

Finally, be patient. Patience is the challenge and the key to being with and moving through dark times. Be as patient as you can be, and be compassionate with yourself for being only as patient as you are.

Let Your Body Guide You

The body is a safe haven, a home base from which we can meet our challenges with grace and clarity. Because it is also a faithful witness, present to everything we experience, it can be an indispensable guide.

Before I say more about this, it feels important to acknowledge that many of us have run roughshod over our bodies, numbing our senses with food or other substances, dulling our awareness with overwork, and ignoring symptoms or turning them off with painkillers.

Some of us have had painful experiences that make the body seem like anything but a safe haven. And then there are the distorted body images that bombard us daily.

Still, here you are, in a body! What an amazing thing that is.

You don't need to have had an idyllic relationship with your body in order to tap into its wisdom now. All that is needed is that you make a beginning, and you can do that by simply being curious about what your dear old body is experiencing as in the following exercise.

Exercise: Finding the Safe Haven

Sit quietly, feet flat on the floor, hands relaxed at your side, back straight and eyes gently closed.

Scan your body for sensations by directing your awareness first to your feet, then to your ankles, calves, knees, thighs, hips, etc. all the way up your body to the crown of your head. As you direct your attention to each area, just observe whatever sensations show up. Don't try to change anything or figure out what the sensations "mean." Just pay attention to how it is with your body right now.

When you have completed the scan, sense into your body for that place where you feel whole and intact. (It can help to recall a time when you felt whole and intact, then notice how you experience that in your body.) Breathe into this place and allow the well being you find there to expand into the rest of your body.

Don't worry if nothing seems to be happening or if you do not seem to understand what "sensing into your body" means. Simply set the intention, spend a few minutes with your body in and attitude of open and interested curiosity, and listen. If you feel discomfort, distraction, or resistance, simply notice that, too. It is all part of the experience of being a body.

30-Second Transformers

The body and mind are interconnected. Simple physical actions can have profound effects on how clearly we think. The following short exercises integrate the right and left hemispheres of the brain, improving attention span, focus, and alertness as well as creativity.

Connecting with your body and doing exercises like these is a good way to change gears when you are going from one kind of task to another. Try doing the transformers before you sit down to write. Spend a few minutes just being with your body before you make an important phone call. Experiment to see how you can best relate to your body as an accidental entrepreneur.

Left and Right

This and the following two practices integrate your nervous system by connecting opposing sides of your body.

Place one hand at the top of your chest with the thumb pressing lightly on a point just below one collarbone where it meets the sternum and the index and middle fingers pressing on the corresponding point just below the other collarbone. At the same time, use the fingers of your other hand to put light pressure on your navel.

Rub the chest points gently for 15 seconds while continuing to press lightly on your navel.

Reverse hands and repeat.

Top and Bottom

Place the thumb of one hand on the depression just below the center of your bottom lip and put the index finger of the same hand on the depression above the center of your upper lip. At the same time, use the fingers of your other hand to put light pressure on your navel.

Hold the lip points for 15 seconds while continuing to press lightly on your navel.

Reverse hands and repeat.

Front and Back

With one hand, gently rub the tip of your coccyx. (This is the bony protuberance below the shallow depression under your tailbone.) At the same time, use the fingers of your other hand to put light pressure on your navel.

Continue to rub the tip of the coccyx for 15 seconds while continuing to press lightly on your navel.

Reverse hands and repeat.

Cross Crawl

I first learned of the power of this technique from Jean Houston, who with her husband, Bob Masters, is a pioneer in the field of human potential. Simply march in place, extending your left arm when you raise your right leg and vice versa. Move slowly and deliberately. Complete 20 full cycles or 40 steps (left arm/right leg plus right arm/left leg).

Hook-ups

Originated by Wayne Cook and modified by Dr. Paul Dennison, this practice is effective in shifting from hyperactivity to a calm and focused state. The exercise is done in a standing position.

Part 1: Cross your left ankle over your right ankle. Extend your arms straight in front of you and cross your wrists, then clasp your hands. Bring your clasped hands in toward your chest and up through your arms until they rest on your chest. Close your eyes. (You may feel that you are swaying. It's okay.)

Remain in this position, breathing slowly and easily, for about one minute.

Part 2: Open your eyes. Uncross your hands and feet. Bring your hands together in front of your belly with your fingers spread and palms apart, forming a sort of triangle. Hold this position, fingertips touching and breathing slowly, for about one minute.

Even before you have completed Part 1, you may become aware of sounds and sensations that you had not been aware of. Hook-ups are a terrific way to come home to yourself.

Thinking Caps

This ear massage feels so good you may find yourself doing it several times a day. It is great for improving your balance.

Take hold of your ear at the top where it meets the side of your face. Gently massage around the ear, using your thumb and forefinger to unfurl the curled edge and continuing to massage until you reach the bottom of the lobe. Repeat three times.

There are more than 140 acupuncture points on the back of the ear, so it's no wonder that this gentle practice generates such a strong feeling of well-being.

Lazy Eights

Even good readers may find that some material is hard to recall. Often this is due to stress related to the topic or context. This brain-body integration practice will help you read more effectively and retain more of what you read even if you have experienced stress related to the subject matter.

Extend your right arm straight in front at the midline of your body. Make a pointer of your index finger, and focus on it throughout the exercise.

Using your finger pointer, draw a lazy eight (a figure 8 on its side). Beginning at the center of the figure, move your finger up to the left, down and around, back to the center, then up to the right, down and around to the center. Draw 20 lazy eights with your right hand, then 20 with your left hand. Finally, extend both hands and use them together to draw 20 more lazy eights.

Emotional Reset

This practice defuses emotional stress. It's interesting to notice that many people do this spontaneously when they are feeling overwhelmed, though most often they do not maintain the movement long enough to receive the full benefit.

Before you begin, notice a stressful memory or thought related to building a business. Observe how you respond to that thought. You may notice tension in your shoulders, a nervous stomach, or other symptoms of stress.

Now, place the palm of one hand over your forehead and the palm of your other hand across the back of your head at the base of the skull. Rest your hands in this position for a minute or so until the stressful sensations are gone. The more intense your stress, the longer this may take.

Hoo-haw

I can understand if this seems like a lot of hoo-haw. Or maybe you don't have any problem with the theory, but aren't too thrilled with the idea of spending five or 10 minutes preparing yourself this way every time you decide to work on your business.

But here's the deal. You can approach business with all your biases, stressful thoughts, and past disappointments intact, or you can start with a clean slate in the here and now. I know from experience that knowing what to do and doing it are two entirely different things. When it comes to your business, it could be the difference between success and failure.

Now that would be worth 10 minutes of your day, don't you think?

Chapter 8

Keep the Channel Open

There is a vitality, a life force, a quickening that is translated through you into action, and because there is only one of you in all time, this expression is unique. And if you block it, it will never exist through any other medium and be lost. The world will not have it. It is not your business to determine how good it is, nor how valuable it is, nor how it compares with other expressions. It is your business to keep it yours clearly and directly, to keep the channel open. You do not even have to believe in yourself or your work. You have to keep yourself open and aware directly to the urges that motivate you. Keep the channel open. ~Martha Graham

The first thing I should say with respect to Keeping the Channel Open is that I'm not terribly good at it. Sometimes the channel is open and sometimes it's not. That made this chapter very difficult to write.

On one hand, I believe that Martha Graham is right. Each of us is a channel through which the life force (or what I've been calling Source) becomes manifest. Though the force is One, it takes on an infinite variety of qualities depending on the channel through which it is translated.

I also knew that Keeping the Channel Open has had everything to do with how I built my business. When I look back on the first years, following this instruction showed me what to do, when to do it, and when to let go.

But when it came to writing about it, my mind went blank. I felt defensive. Then I got irritated. "What part of Keep the Channel Open don't they understand?" I complained to my editor, only half joking. Finally, I resorted to the first instruction and questioned my thoughts.

Judging You, Dear Reader

I wrote out my judgments about writing this section. Most of them were unwelcome because they consisted of thoughts that I didn't want to believe. Once again I learned that thoughts don't go away just because I find them beneath my dignity.

At first, I couldn't see any judgments that weren't about me. I'm the one who was stuck. I'm the one who was cranky and defensive. I'm the one who doesn't have the right to teach anyone else about Keeping the Channel Open.

And then I felt the familiar sensation of being snagged by a seemingly sensible belief, in this case, the belief that you needed to be taught.

They need me to teach them. Is it true? *No. I can't know that.*

How do I react when I believe that thought? What happens? *I question every word I write to find out if it could possibly be misunderstood. I second-guess myself. Who am I to suggest that my experience and perspectives are "right"? What if I offend someone from a different spiritual tradition? Will that make the whole book irrelevant to them? I put lots of pressure on me to get this right—so much pressure that I can hardly move.*

I also feel tremendous pressure to make this work for people. When I think that they need me to teach them, I worry that they won't succeed and that it will be my fault. Then I start feeling trapped and resentful. I imagine readers unwilling to do what it takes to make this section meaningful for their own lives. The more I worry, the less I think of my readers, and that makes me worry even more.

Who would I be without this thought? *Telling my story. Humble. Grateful. Excited about putting this out into the world and letting it go. Excited about what others will do with it once it is in their hands. Curious. And much, much more light-hearted. Oh—and open. Willing to make a mistake because curiosity and enthusiasm will be more relevant than being right.*

Turnarounds for "They need me to teach them."

They don't need me to teach them. This is at least as true and probably truer. I'm writing for people who are self-aware and committed to their own growth. They can teach themselves.

I need me to teach them. This is truer, especially when my ego gets involved. I need me to teach them when I am attached to being right. I'm the one who puts me in the position of authority; I make myself the responsible big sister running everyone's life. Ouch!

I need them to teach me. Yes. This feels most true. All through the writing process, readers have been teaching me. They've taught me patience. They've taught me that I am not alone, that they support me spiritually and emotionally, not just economically. Time and again they teach me that I don't serve by being perfect or right but by being real. They are also teaching me to admit that I am human and deal with it.

And with that, I was ready to get back to writing.

Allowing

Next, I turned to the dictionary. I looked up the definition of *open* and found that the first word was "allowing."

Open: allowing access, passage, or a view through an empty space; not closed or blocked up

Yes. We Keep the Channel Open when we allow for insight, support, grace, and happy accident. When we open ourselves to what is, allowing Reality to refine and reshape our ambitions and our plans, we become truly powerful.

Allowing gives us power *for*, not power *over*. To allow is to say yes to an invitation to the cosmic dance. The price for partnering with this greater power is surrender of our puny power. That requires courage, humility, and creative vision.

The G-Word

In addition to being confused about the teaching thing, I found writing about Keeping the Channel Open difficult because I was worried about how people would respond to the G-word, God. I might as well just admit that God and I are in a long-term, if non-traditional, relationship.

I was born a Roman Catholic and attended parochial schools through high school except for a brief hiatus in 5th and 6th grade. (Don't ask me how, but my 7th grade teacher, Sister Mary Benedict, noticed immediately. "Did you transfer from public school?" she asked.)

Like many long-term relationships, the one between God and me began with heartfelt sighs and longing gazes, then went downhill. We've fought, made-up, and renegotiated our relationship so many times I have lost track. Some days God and I are an old married couple. I roll my eyes at His eccentricities and excesses. He remains maddeningly placid, almost patronizing. (I hate that) Other days it's as if time and the world have vanished and we are utterly lost in each other, bedazzled and dizzy as young lovers.

As you can tell, personifying Source is second nature for me. I understand that it doesn't work for everyone, nor does it need to. Still, a personal God is at the heart of my tradition. Something in me shrivels when I get on my existential high horse and deny His existence. My life works better when I believe.

It is up to you to find your own story of Source, a story that provides a way to imagine yourself as a channel. When that channel is open, you are free from the need to know more, be more, or do more than you can. At the same time, infinite Source is expressed through you in ways that will never happen otherwise.

It's All Connected

As human beings, we have many ways of experiencing ourselves in the world. We use language to explain and communicate our experience, and language also shapes our perceptions. Emotion arises from experience, and it also colors our interpretations and reactions. The body experiences and responds to the world, and what happens in the body has a lot to do with how we perceive and interact with that world.

It's all connected.

The intricate and perhaps infinite interplay of what we experience and what we perceive has implications for keeping the channel open. The way we think, speak, act, and feel has everything to do with the results we experience. There are countless opportunities for us to consciously participate in creating our lives, ranging from how we eat to the company we keep to the goals we set.

Creating

Human beings have an innate need to create, a drive to bring new ideas, new life, new possibilities into the world. But to create is not to control, as any artist can tell you. That's because all creation is actually co-creation.

What we create begins to push back almost from the moment we begin. As a sculptor chips away at the marble surface, he sees in the stone a curve, a shadow, a gesture that he had not imagined. The novelist finds that her characters have developed minds of their own, declining to behave in the way she had planned.

Likewise, when you grow a business, things don't always go the way you thought you wanted them to. Your business cards are lost in transit; the phone lines go down before a crucial call; or you become ill and cannot make a deadline. You can regard such surprises as cruel tricks of fate, or you can meet them with the eyes and heart of an artist locked in deep conversation with her work.

Whose Business Are You In?

Byron Katie says there are only three kinds of business in the world: my business, your business, and God's business. (Katie equates God with Reality.) Being in anyone's business but my own is crazy-making because I have no power there. The only place I have power is in my own business.

When you're in someone else's business, you feel insecure, uncertain, less-than because you have no firm basis for believing or disbelieving your thoughts. No matter how vivid and convincing your experiences are when you are in someone else's business, they are always based on guesswork. You just can't know how it is for anyone else but you.

Being in someone else's business is frustrating, even maddening. No matter how hard you push, things don't always go the way you want them to.

One of the most painful ways to be in someone else's business is comparing yourself to them. Comparing someone's outsides to your insides will make you nuts. How can you know what is really going on for anyone else? For all you know, the person you envy is being sued for back taxes and the person you pity is blissfully happy.

When you're in your business, you feel at home, safe and secure. That's because you *are* at home, present to your self in the moment, undistracted by arguments with Reality.

All About You

As Martha Graham said with respect to the work you produce, "It is not your business to determine how good it is, nor how valuable it is, nor how it compares with other expressions." Graham continues, "It is your business to keep it yours clearly and directly, to keep the channel open. You do not even have to believe in yourself or your work. You have to keep yourself open and aware directly to the urges that motivate you."

That can be confusing. On one hand, you have limited control over how the work goes and it's not your business anyway. On the other, you are supposed to pay attention to the urges that motivate you to do the work. In other words, go for what you want, just don't expect it to go the way you want.

It's a lot like walking in the fog.

In Praise of Fog

It may be that when we no longer know what to do, we have come to our real work, and that when we no longer know which way to go, we have begun our real journey. The mind that is not baffled is not employed. The impeded stream is the one that sings. ~Wendell Berry

One day when I was trying to write a business plan but kept getting stuck, I was struck suddenly by the image of being lost in a thick bank of fog. This was not a mist, softening the edges of the world around me, but pea soup, utterly impenetrable.

It seemed to me that the fog was related to my struggles with planning. It might have served simply to validate my frustration, proving, after a fashion, that I didn't know what to do next. But I didn't need a spontaneous image to tell me that. So I got curious.

I went into the image, and looked for more information. It came to me that I was standing in a meadow on a cliff overlooking the sea. I didn't know how far I was from the edge of the cliff. I listened to see if the sound of the surf could orient me, but it was distorted by the swirling fog. I wasn't even certain in what direction the cliff lay.

I continued to explore my imaginary situation, watching it unfold as if it were a movie. I became aware of the sensation of the fog against my skin. I noticed the feeling of my feet in their heavy boots. I realized that while I could not see farther than my outstretched hand, I was quite safe.

I actually held my arm out as if to make out my hand. In that simple gesture, I realized that I was not only safe, I had plenty of information available for this moment. So long as I used my sense of touch to test the ground and paid keen attention to what I could see, I could navigate.

I tell this story for two reasons: to illustrate one way that I practice Keeping the Channel Open and to show you that being lost in the fog can be a very good place to be.

Time and again, working for ourselves puts us in unfamiliar and confusing situations. Sometimes we don't have the information or support we think we need. But we always have exactly what we need for the task at hand. It's only when we insist on walking faster than conditions allow that we are in danger.

The following visualization can give you a felt sense of how you can relate to confusion and not knowing.

Visualization: Wrapped in Safety

If you can, have a friend or study partner read the visualization. You might also record it for yourself.

Imagine a slightly misty plateau high above the ocean. It is morning. You are standing a fair distance from the cliff, though you can still hear the sounds of the surf.

As the warmth of the morning sun meets the cool ground, the mist becomes a warm, dense fog, veiling the landscape.

As you stand enveloped in the fog, you might let your awareness settle into your body. Notice the soles of your feet pressing on the earth. Feel the support.

You open your arms and begin to sway. In a moment, with a deep sigh, your body comes to rest. You are so very present, so very safe.

You gently probe the ground with your feet—so much information! How can you be lost while you are able to touch the earth this way?

You extend an arm in front of you, and you notice that you can see your outstretched hand. And now you see with your inner eyes that you will always be given everything you need to take one step.

One step. And then you might pause, sensing the warm embrace of the fog. It is so good to be here, to be held this way.

And now you put out your hand again. Feeling the earth beneath your feet, you take a baby step.

Practice: Instrument Rules

Not all who wander are lost. ~ J.R. Tolkien

Though we may move with care through a fog bank, as accidental entrepreneurs we can rarely afford to stop altogether. When pilots need to navigate through heavy clouds, they stop using visual flight rules and start using their instruments. I like to think of the following practice as the accidental entrepreneur's equivalent of instrument rules.* When you are faced with a big decision and don't know which way is the right way, this practice can help. You will need a notebook and pen and a quiet place to sit at the end of the day.

First, identify the situation about which you want guidance. Here are some examples of situations my clients have chosen.

Hiring employees or other support staff.

Beginning or ending a partnership or collaboration.

---

* If you are familiar with the Spiritual Exercises of Ignatius of Loyola, you may recognize this practice as an adaptation of the Examen.

Changing the focus of one's work.

Buying new equipment.

Borrowing money.

Though the daily commitment to this practice is only 5 or 10 minutes, the process takes at least a month. That's because you will need several weeks to observe patterns or tendencies in the subtle movements of Spirit in your life. Make a commitment to a specific period of practice from 30 to 90 days.

At the end of each day, go to a quiet place where you will not be disturbed. You might light a candle or play some music to establish a boundary between this sacred time and the rest of your day.

Take a few minutes to get quiet and centered. Allow the concerns, ambitions, and distractions of the day to drop away. Ground yourself in the presence of a loving Source. (You do not need to believe in a conventional God to use this process effectively. It does help to acknowledge that there are forces at work in the Universe that are more powerful than you are.)

Invite into your awareness the time in your day when you were most aware of being a Channel for Source. You might think of this as a time when you felt something light you up. Sometimes it helps to think of this as a moment when you experienced great peace, gratitude, or joy. Take a minute to recollect this moment as fully as you can, recalling the physical sensation and mental and emotional state that you experienced. When you are ready, jot down a few words to mark this experience. Draw a circle around what you wrote.

Next, invite into your awareness the time in your day when you felt least aware of being a Channel or when you felt blocked, inhibited, or closed to Source. This could be a moment when you felt ill-at-ease, dissatisfied, or frustrated. Sit with your recollection without judgment, simply noticing what was going on and how it was for you. When you are ready, jot down a few words to capture the experience. Surround the words with a jagged star.

Each day, add to this simple log. When you finish your entries for the day, offer a brief prayer of gratitude. You might also ask for guidance and for the grace to receive it.

At the end of the time you set (at least 30 days), go to your quiet place to review your notes. You will want at least 30 minutes for this. Again, get quiet and invite Source to be with you. You might use the body scan or a few of the transformers to help you settle and be present. (See Finding the Safe Haven, page 49, and 30 Second Transformers, beginning on page 50.)

When you feel ready, page through your log from the beginning. Notice any patterns that might help you make a good decision. For example, if you notice that your times of greatest connection and joy almost always involved collaboration, you may question whether taking on an extended solo project is right for you.

After you have completed your review, sit in silence for at least 15 minutes. Let your mind be as empty as possible, and when you find your attention drifting, gently bring it back to the present. At the end of your time, say a prayer of gratitude.

The following section explains in more detail how observing what lights us up can help us grow businesses that fit just-right.

Desire as an Ally

We are told that talent creates its own opportunities. But it sometimes seems that intense desire creates not only its own opportunities, but its own talents. ~Eric Hoffer

Desire can be our greatest ally in Keeping the Channel Open. Much of western culture sees desire as all about getting what we want. If we fulfill a desire, we feel great. If we fail to fulfill a desire, we feel lousy.

But in terms of the Channel, desire is not about getting what is desired but about following clues in a treasure hunt. What we desire is not the object of the journey but a lodestone, a pole whose magnetic field is a navigational aide, showing us in which direction to move now.

Doing the work of knowing what we want is about reading a compass as we travel uncharted territory. "This way," prompts desire, and we take a few steps, testing the wisdom and accuracy of our readings by noticing the results. Perhaps we follow a desire for a few hours or days, and then another desire kicks in, inviting us to turn or to look in a new direction.

This interpretation of desire requires passion, commitment, humility, flexibility. It requires that we be willing to tend to our desires, moving toward them and then letting go of them when we get new "directions." It asks us to "not know" while staying wide-awake.

Just as an electromagnetic field from a power station can throw off a compass, some desires are distractions or seductions that take us away from our path. Working with desire as a navigational aid means constantly checking to see if we are moving toward or away from the qualities and virtues that make our lives meaningful.

Though desire rarely traces a direct path through the unknown, the unfolding of desire can be a through-line, an invisible yet palpable thread through which we feel our way as the path emerges. When we are at an edge, our destination is unknown. Desire affords us the opportunity to wander in new territory while remaining oriented to what is calling us forward.

Passion

Sometimes we confuse Keeping the Channel Open with living our passion. It seems that everyone wants to tap into their passion, create work they feel passionate about, or express their passion. But where does passion really fit in the journey to a business that fits just-right?

If you're assuming that just-right and a business you're passionate about are the same thing, think again. There are several ways that passion can derail your business, not to mention obstruct your personal growth and genuine channel to the Source.

Passion is defined as a strong and barely controllable emotion.* It has its roots in the relationship between suffering and creating meaning. (The root is *pati*, Latin for "suffer." The Passion is a central teaching in Christian theology.) I'm not against suffering per se (it may be optional, but that doesn't render it valueless or mean that if you suffer you are some kind of spiritual nitwit). But do you really want to grow a business out of your commitment to suffering?

Another way passion can derail us is by requiring our work to provide most of our emotional and spiritual nourishment. This places a huge burden on even a mature and healthy business, a burden that can strangle a new business before it can take root.

Growing a business is a lot like starting a family. Parenthood can bring enormous emotional and spiritual gratification, but it's of the character-building kind. The work of being a parent is never done, and the primary flow of nourishment is from parent to child, not vice versa. If you require your children to meet your deepest emotional and spiritual needs, you and they will suffer greatly.

---

* *Oxford American Dictionary*

The nourishment we can expect of our businesses is also of the character-building kind. We can expect our businesses to push our buttons so that we can see what work there is to be done on the inside. We can expect our businesses to be the means through which we serve others in return for financial compensation. We can require our businesses to operate in alignment with our ethics.

But if we expect our businesses to make us feel good, or to feed and be fueled by passion, we're setting ourselves up for disappointment.

The Role of Emotion in Business

This is not to say that there is no place for emotion in business. For one thing, emotion is unavoidable. For another, emotion is what moves us into action. (The Latin root of emotion means "to move out.")

Emotions precede movement; they predispose us to act in certain ways. When we feel anger, we are predisposed to strike out. When we feel fear we are predisposed to defend. When we feel joy, we are predisposed to celebrate.

As we mature, emotion becomes a teacher rather than a dictator. It continues to provide an important impetus to action, but we get to choose the degree to which the action is determined by our emotional state. We develop the ability to shift emotional states intentionally in service of our values and goals. Far from being inauthentic, this ability is part of what raises living to the level of art.

Should You or Shouldn't You?

The dictionary says that "should" expresses obligation or duty, and that's where things can get dicey. Obligation or duty to whom? To what?

When the channel that connects us with Source is open, we may feel a sort of inner mandate to act in accordance with the guidance we receive. This kind of "should" urges us in the direction that is right for us. When we honor these "shoulds," we thrive spiritually as well as materially.

Other "shoulds" lead to war with the self. Believing that I should be more outgoing at networking breakfasts will just make me miserable if, in fact, I am not outgoing.

Here are two ways to explore your "shoulds" so you can honor inner mandates without arguing with yourself or Reality.

Word Play

Play with changing "should" to "need," "must," or "want" Watch what happens in your body and emotions as you try on these different meanings. Does one of them feel truer? How would you live the "must"? The "could"?

I used to be at war with filing. Whenever I'd add a document to the pile on my desk, I would think, "I should file that."

So I tried, "I need to file that." Well, that was obviously not true. The world would not come to an end if I didn't.

Then I tried, "I must file." This could be true. My practice was to let things pile up until they bothered me, and then I'd put them away. If the only thing bothering me was the "should," the filing could wait.

And I tried, "I want to file that." That led me to inquire, "Do I want it filed?" If yes, then I can file it. If no, then I can let it go.

Exercise: Should Play

Make a list of the "shoulds" that are on your mind right now.

Backtrack

"Shoulds" are only problematic when they lead to inner combat. Go inside, and trace your "should" back to the beginning. See if you can notice where the thought started and when you started to debate it. Is there any peaceful reason not to follow the promptings of the original thought?

Again, let's look at my war with filing. I'd think, "I should catch up on filing," and immediately the debate would begin.

"Why? Who says?" I'd go round and round until I was either sick of myself or exhausted, and then I'd be certain that "shoulding" was my problem.

But "shoulding" was not the problem. The problem was that, instead of questioning the thought, I argued with it.

Anyone who has asked for clarification can attest to the difference between questioning and arguing. "Do you really need this by Friday?" is not the same as "Since when do you get to tell me what to do?" Questioning is respectful, open-minded. Arguing is disrespectful and close-minded.

"Shoulds" may be mandates from your heart or random thoughts, perfectly innocent until you begin to debate with them. Knowing the difference lends dignity to your choices without making you a slave to perfection.

Exercise: Backtracking

Choose one of the shoulds from your list. Answer the following questions.

1. **Where and when did the thought first occur?**
2. **When did you begin to debate the thought?**

3. **Is there a peaceful reason not to follow the promptings of the thought?**

Self Care and the Channel

Self-care is fundamental to keeping your channel open. Is self-care something you practice based on how well you have behaved or performed lately or how much you have left to do? If so, you run the risk of running out of gas in the middle of the night on a deserted highway.

The image is vivid, yet it can still be difficult to care for ourselves and for each other when we are caught in a frantic pattern of busyness. It can even be hard to get enough perspective to acknowledge that we are running in circles and on empty.

I'm no stranger to these difficulties, and I have good news. Even the most frenetic busybody can learn to treat herself at least as well as she would treat her car.

Make a list of things that fill your tank, without which you cannot expect to function as a loving human being. For example: Exercise; eating well; prayer and meditation; petting the cat; eight hours of sleep. If you are really stuck in busy-ness, ask a friend to gently point out what you are overlooking.

Keeping gas in the tank is a non-negotiable precondition to being able to drive. It needs to be tended to every day. Take a few minutes to fully appreciate that when you skip these things you are running on fumes. With this in mind, make the decision that these tank-filling activities are the functional equivalent of work and will no longer be treated as optional extras or self-indulgence.

Make a list of things that are akin to getting the oil changed in your car. These do not need to be tended to as often, and when you are honest with yourself, you will find that you know what the appropriate intervals are. Schedule them into your calendar and keep your commitments. Breaking these commitments reduces the life of your engine! Examples might include getting a bi-weekly massage or having your teeth cleaned every six months.

List those things that are the equivalent of getting a car wash. Strictly speaking, these items may not have a direct effect on your car's performance, but it sure seems to run better and it is definitely more fun to drive. (In my family, we call a good car wash the poor man's tune-up.) For me, a visit to the hot tubs, a pedicure, or a haircut fall into this category.

The above examples are of personal self-care. How about doing this exercise with your mate or with the whole family as the basis for setting priorities for the coming year?

Chapter 9

Calling Your Energy Home

Working for yourself takes a lot of time and energy. This chapter provides remedies for two of the primary causes of low energy: leakage and distraction. These usually occur together: we leak energy to unimportant activities or subconscious commitments as a result of failing to focus our intentions and make considered choices.

The simple (if not easy) solution is to call our energy home by noticing where it is going and then redirecting it in ways that support our real values and intentions. This Keeps the Channel Open.

Call your energy home with an energy inventory. As you read the following questions, notice if you are losing energy in that area. Simply notice without judgment, holding yourself whole, competent, and resourceful to redirect your energy when you choose to do so.

Unfinished Business

☐ Are my bank accounts balanced and all transactions current?

☐ Do I have unresolved conflicts with a friend or family member?

☐ Do I have unresolved conflicts with someone at work?

☐ Am I behind on my debts? Do I know exactly what I owe and to whom?

☐ Do I have an overdue assignment?

☐ Do I have incomplete projects at home? at work? in my community?

☐ Is there a phone call or letter that I have delayed answering?

Physical Environment

☐ Does my household environment express and support my intentions?

☐ Does my work environment express and support my intentions?

☐ Is my car (bike) clean and in good repair?

☐ Is my equipment in good repair?

☐ Are there chores that I have been putting off?

Support Systems

☐ In what ways do I give and receive energy with my family?

☐ Do I give and receive energy in friendship in a healthy way?

☐ In what ways am I giving and receiving energy with my spouse/partner?

☐ Do I know where to get help and do I ask for help when I need it?

Physical Health

☐ Have I been putting off a physical or other health care service?

☐ Do I sustain my energy and well being with exercise?

☐ Do I eat in a way that supports a stable and high level of energy?

☐ Do I get enough sleep?

Mental, Emotional, and Spiritual Health

☐ Do I owe an apology or have amends to make?

☐ Am I holding on to resentment?

☐ Is there someone I need to forgive?

☐ What spiritual practice am I doing on a regular basis to center and renew me?

☐ Am I learning something new?

☐ Am I interested and engaged in my work?

When you have identified your energy leaks, you will begin to recognize ways to close them. Each time you close an energy leak you become more focused and clear. You'll notice a more open channel of inspiration flowing. Be patient, be honest, and you will soon develop the momentum to live your life in a more satisfying manner.

Clearing a Way

Your energy inventory may reveal a heap of half-completed projects and loose ends that are cluttering up your mind and your office. These can put a serious crimp in the channel between you and your clients, not to mention you and your Source. Here's one way to clear a way through the mess.

1. Make a list of the projects and tasks that are incomplete. Don't bother to prioritize. Just get it all down.

   When you have a list, sort it into these categories:

   • Things you never really wanted to do and don't honestly care about. (If necessary, do The Work on the thoughts that would keep you from crossing these off your list.)

   • Commitments that won't go away because they matter to you. (If the only reason they matter is because of what someone else may think, do The Work.)

   • Commitments that matter and need immediate attention.

2. Throw away, give away, recycle, or put away visible traces of anything you don't really need to do and won't do.

3. Get out your calendar and block out time to complete the remaining projects. If you are not sleep-deprived, consider getting up an hour earlier until you catch up.

4. Schedule time to complete important recurring tasks such as filing quarterly taxes, balancing your checking account, sending out invoices.

Remember, you are an adult and you have some choices. Hire help or exchange tasks with a friend or colleague, assigning each other jobs that you are each well-equipped to handle and handing off the ones you don't do well or at all. Examine the standards you set yourself: do you set up unnecessarily complicated systems or such high standards that finishing a project is nearly impossible? (Uh-oh. I'm projecting again. You can call me the queen of complication.)

Over-Committed and Under-Powered

When we work for ourselves, we may over-commit, losing energy to overwhelm, over-work, and self-criticism. That leaves us under-powered. Being under-powered can leave us too frazzled to even figure out a routine for recharging.

There's no shortage of advice for managing time and commitments, and that can actually make things worse. How do you decide which advice to take? Where do you start? Who do you trust?

If that's happening for you, choose one—and only one—strategy from the list below and use it for 21 days.

We have a tendency to complicate things when we are overwhelmed. To help you keep it simple, there are examples for how to use each strategy.

1. **Walk your talk.** Take a walk daily, rain or shine.

   Julia got stuck trying to schedule 20 minutes every day. She got unstuck when she decided to walk for no longer than 10 minutes before she went into her office.

2. **Order the chaos.** Spend 30 minutes every day putting something in order, such as cleaning a closet, filing personal papers, or balancing your checkbook. Break big jobs down into smaller ones.

   Mark didn't know where to begin. His coach suggested he start with his sock drawer. It sounds silly, but it got him started. Being in action felt good, and Mark realized that taking action was more important at that time than prioritizing.

3. **Meditate.** For centuries wise and healthy people have used meditation to cultivate presence and equanimity. I recommend Lawrence Le Shan's simple, secular guide, *How to Meditate.*

4. **Say "I don't know."** If you get roped in because you always have or are willing to find answers, practice saying, "I don't know." Not only will this reduce the number of "little things" you volunteer to do, it will help break the addiction to being right.

    Alicia didn't like the idea of saying she didn't know if she did. I asked her to commit to listening very carefully when she was asked a question and to stop herself unless she truly knew the answer. She was astonished to discover how many questions she tried to answer with speculation.

5. **Practice answering requests with, "I'll get back to you."** Whenever you are asked to quote a fee for a new project, specify a completion date, or bake cookies for school, say, "Can I get back to you on that?" This gives you time to think through your commitments before you make them. It is also a simple way to keep other people's urgency from becoming your emergency.

    Marilyn had a pattern of agreeing to far more than she could do. When she gave herself a day to consider requests, she was able to see which ones really mattered. She also realized how much her self-image was tied up with doing things for others. It took a while, but in time she was able to distinguish truly important commitments from unnecessary ones.

Entrepreneurs Who Work Too Much

Another trap for the accidental entrepreneur is working too many hours with too little to show for it. The less satisfied we feel with our output, the harder we work. After a certain point, more work just depletes our confidence, energy and self-esteem.

The solution? Put banks on the river. Set hours, even arbitrary ones, for starting and stopping work. Then follow them, one day at a time, for a week. By the end of seven days you will start to feel more effective and resilient.

Here are some additional tips for adding structure when work takes over. Remember, structure is meant to support you, not imprison you. It takes about 21 days to establish a habit, so practice a new strategy for three weeks. Then you can decide if it is a keeper.

Work when you say you're going to work.

This means getting rid of distractions. Dump the computer game that pulls you away from your next task. Check your email once in the morning and once in the afternoon instead of every 15 minutes. Let voice mail take your calls and return them once a day.

Play when you say you're going to play.

No fluffing up the mailing list while you listen to the radio. No editing a report while you sit in the tub or watch TV.

Get enough sleep.

Even subtle sleep deprivation makes it difficult for you to concentrate on work and robs your play-time of vigor.

Be realistic when making commitments.

Use a planner and mark out personal time so that you don't inadvertently promise to deliver work that will require you to give up a day off.

Getting Clients

Demystifying the Client Relationship

What is the difference between commercial and social relationships? How does this affect the process of getting and keeping clients? What customs and practices do people need to do business with each other? As you answer these questions for yourself, you are likely to find that you are actually very well qualified to start and maintain enjoyable relationships with your just-right clients.

Clients are people. They have talents and weaknesses, good days and bad days, likes and dislikes. In many respects, getting clients is no more mysterious than making friends. That said, the relationships we have with clients is not the same as the ones we have with friends and acquaintances. The most obvious difference is that commercial relationships involve the exchange of products and services for money or some other form of compensation.

Business Is Business

The difference between commercial and social relationships is money. We don't usually pay our friends to come over for tea or our families for hosting the Thanksgiving meal. What makes a client a client and a customer a customer is that they pay us.

While paying money (or something of equal value) is a prerequisite for a commercial relationship, it is not enough. Relationships develop over time through multiple transactions—

not all of them monetary. And for our relationships with clients and customers to feel "just-right," those transactions need to feel good. That means they have to feel safe.

Safety First

Safety is important even in personal relationships, and it is essential in all but the most trivial business transactions. That's because money is not just a store of value; it is a form of life energy. When we spend money, we are putting a lot on the line: our values, priorities, resources, self-image, social standing, and more. This is true both for us and for clients and customers.

When we feel vulnerable, especially in unfamiliar situations, we often feel afraid. When we are afraid, our minds go looking for an explanation. If we don't question these explanations ("She won't want to pay that much," for example, or "He just wants to make a sale,") they turn into evidence that there really is something to fear.

This creates a feedback loop, a self-reinforcing system of beliefs. Our unquestioned explanations for feeling vulnerable keeps us from noticing that clients are people, just like us.

The good news is that these feedback loops also contain everything we need to know to communicate with just-right clients and customers. All we need to do (remember, this is simple, not easy) is to notice the ways in which we and our clients or customers are vulnerable, acknowledge the vulnerability, and respond to it with appropriate reassurances and options.

The Three Instructions can interrupt this kind of feedback loop about attracting just-right clients.

1. **Question Stressful Thoughts:** Notice how you explain the difficulty of getting clients to yourself and question those explanations.

2. **Be Yourself:** Play with ways to relate to clients that are good for you, for them, and for your business.

3. **Keep the Channel Open:** Cultivate receptivity and open-minded curiosity so that Source can work through you and support you.

Exercise: The Habit of Safety

Our bodies store patterns of response to both safety and fear. When you step out of your comfort zone, your body may default to a pattern of fear. Even if you are mentally prepared, this fear patterning can take over.

You can train yourself to observe the differences between how your body is when you are afraid and when you feel safe. Then you will notice when a fear pattern gets triggered, and you can intervene.

This exercise develops your ability to notice and shift your state. If you are not accustomed to this kind of noticing, be kind to yourself. Go through the steps and don't worry about doing it right. (You can't do it wrong, so long as you do it.) Learning to notice this way is a matter of practice. They pay-off is better follow through when you've decided to step out of your comfort zone.

The Experience of Fear

Bring to mind a specific fear related to getting clients. Notice what happens. Feel how your body responds. What happens to your breathing and posture? What sensations are you aware of? Give yourself plenty of time to be curious in a detached sort of way.

Look for specific sensations ("my stomach is tight"). If you find yourself going to feelings instead of sensations, see where in your body that feeling is showing up. ("I feel irritated. I guess that shows up in my tight jaw and shoulders.")

Make a few notes, then walk around the room before you take the next step.

The Experience of Safety

Think of a time when you felt very confident and safe. As you remember it, notice how your body responds. What happens to your breathing and posture? What sensations are you aware of? Give yourself plenty of time to be curious in a detached sort of way.

Look for specific sensations ("my throat feels warm"). If you find yourself going to feelings instead of sensations, see where in your body that feeling is showing up. ("I feel happy. I guess that shows up in my chest; it feels fluttery, but in a nice way.")

Make a few notes about what you observe.

Practice Safety

Have you ever replayed a scary experience over and over again, feeling almost as frightened as you were when it happened? Or imagined being in a scary situation and feeling anxious and tense? When you think about it, you'll probably discover that you are pretty good at practicing being afraid.

Your body doesn't have an opinion about whether you practice fear or safety, so why not practice safety instead?

You can practice feeling safe in scary situations by remembering what safety feels like in your body. Naturally, you wouldn't do this if you were in mortal danger, but I don't know of a single instance of injury or death related to talking with clients.

Notice the physical sensations that arise when you feel afraid. Use the notes you made in this exercise to remind yourself how it feels to be safe. You can also simply get quiet, close your eyes, and let your body show you how it would be to feel safe right now.

Rehearse. Practice imaginary conversations with clients and prospective clients while you feel safe. Start by getting quiet and imagining yourself utterly safe and secure. You can use your notes to remind you of how your body is when you feel safe. You can also ask your body show to you how safety feels.

When you feel nice and safe, start imagining the conversation. Let one part of you be the observer who notices if you start to go into fear. If this happens, ask your body to show you again how it is to be safe. The more opportunities you have to shift from fear to safety, the better you will get at it.

5 Things Clients and Customers Want

Clients aren't really mysterious. If you can give people these things, they'll love doing business with you. Just remember, it's not about convincing people that you do these things. When you reach out to the just-right client, doing these things just feels right.

1. To know what you can do to make their life better.
2. To be able to find out what it takes to do business with you without a lot of hassle and hype.
3. To take a test drive without getting a hard sell.
4. To compensate you for what they get so they needn't feel obligated and they can feel good about asking for more.
5. To know that you love what you are doing for them.

Example: Judging People Who Don't Get It

My client Andrew wrote a Judge Your Neighbor worksheet on clients who didn't appreciate his work. As you read it, notice where you have had the same thoughts.

1. **Who angers, disappoints, or confuses you, and why? What is it about them that you don't like?**

   I'm angry and confused by people who don't appreciate my work and think I charge too much.

2. **How do you want them to change? What do you want them to do?**

   I want them to appreciate my work. I want them to trust my good intentions.

3. **What is it that they should or shouldn't do, be, think or feel? What advice could you offer?**

   They shouldn't assume that I am pressuring them. They should keep an open mind.

4. **Do you need anything from them? What do they need to do in order for you to be happy?**

   I need them to respect me. I need them to listen to what I tell them.

5. **What do you think of them? Make a list.**

   I think they are mistrustful, cheap, and want something for nothing.

6. **What is it that you never want to experience with this person(s) again?**

   I never want to feel like they don't trust me again.

In the example below you will see how one person took a thought from their Judge Your Neighbor worksheet to Inquiry.

Example: Doing The Work on People Who Don't Get It

As you read the following self-facilitation, put yourself in Andrew's position. Go inside at each of the questions to find your answers. Please take your time. Refer to the instructions in Chapter 5, Questioning Stressful Thoughts.

Andrew answered the first question on the Judge Your Neighbor worksheet like this:

I'm angry and confused by people who don't appreciate my work and think I charge too much.

The Work works best when we keep it simple, so I helped him break this down into two statements to investigate separately.

They don't appreciate my work.

People think I charge too much.

Andrew began with the concept, **"They don't appreciate my work."**

1. **Is it true?**

   It feels like it.

2. **Can I absolutely know that it is true?**

   No. Not absolutely.

3. **How do I react when I believe that thought? What happens?**

   I feel irritable and defensive. I feel angry. I resent them for wasting my time. I feel like quitting. My jaw and the back of my neck get tight. I feel frustrated. I see myself having to convince people I'm not even sure I like to hire me.

4. **Who would I be without this thought?**

   When I imagine talking to them without this thought I am really interested in what they are saying. I feel curious.

Turnarounds for "They don't appreciate my work."

Turn around to the opposite: They do appreciate my work.

This could be as true. Maybe they were asking questions because they appreciate my work. They took the trouble to ask me about my rates. They thanked me.

Turn around to the other: I don't appreciate their work.

Well, I don't appreciate the work they do to learn about what I do and what I charge. I don't appreciate their work of assessing when I think they don't appreciate mine. I don't appreciate their work when I think talking to them has been a waste of time.

Turn around to the self: I don't appreciate my work.

Yes. I see this. I don't appreciate my work when I evaluate it only in terms of how much someone wants to pay. I don't appreciate my work when I imagine that I am being pushy or intrusive by answering questions about it. I don't appreciate my work when I act like I have to defend it to other people. I don't appreciate my work when I don't talk about it frankly and generously.

From Inquiry to Action

Let the beauty you love be what you do. ~Rumi

What do you do when you've finished a worksheet? How do you go from questioning your stressful thoughts about clients to being more effective at actually getting clients?

An effective bridge from Inquiry to action, specifically action that is right for you (Be Yourself), is to ask and answer this question: *How would I live my life differently without this thought?*

Here's what Andrew wrote when I asked him this question.

Without this thought, I wouldn't be trying to read their minds. I'd take questions at face value. It would be natural to answer them, and I wouldn't be paranoid about whether or not people are really interested. Assuming I value my work, there would be no reason not to share it enthusiastically when people ask me about it. Also, my appreciation for my work wouldn't depend on their reaction, so I would be more open and warm and less defensive.

Crossing the Bridge

We cross the bridge from Inquiry to action by imagining what it would be like to live from beliefs that are truer to us than the stressful ones we're used to. A related approach is to think of someone who is successful at getting clients, and to ask ourselves what we would need to believe in order to act like them without being phony.

Bring that effective person to mind. Notice how they hold themselves when they talk about their work. Pay attention to their tone of voice and facial expressions. As you watch, notice any judgments that come up. For example, as I imagine someone being very persuasive, I may have the thought that they care more about making the sale than about serving the customer.

The next step is to become curious about our judgments. (Are you noticing a pattern here?) It helps to observe someone else's way of relating to customers to uncover our own hidden reservations about effective ways to relate to our just-right clients.

Let's imagine Jane, someone who seems to really appreciate the value of her work and isn't afraid to show it. We see Jane in our mind's eye enthusiastically talking to prospective clients. She is animated. She asks questions, probing for what the prospective client needs. When she's asked about her fees, she asks another question before answering. When she does state her fee, she does it clearly and confidently, without apology. If a prospect seems uncomfortable with the price, she asks if they have a concern about the price and, if so, what it is.

As we observe Jane, we might notice that we have thoughts like these:

She's good at convincing people (and I'm not).

She's mostly interested in making the sale (and not in the client's well being).

She's cagey about her price, and that means she's tricking people into making a commitment before they know what it will cost (and I don't want to do that).

She puts people on the spot (and that's mean).

The Switcheroo

Now (surprise, surprise!), we go inside and ask if our thoughts are necessarily true. Sometimes The Work you have already done will cause your thoughts to unravel without even asking the four questions. In that case your process might look something like this.

She's good at convincing people (and I'm not).

When am I convincing? What does it take for me to feel good about being convincing? And is this really about "convincing"? What if it's about being clear about how I could help? And if I trust people to make the right decision for themselves, why wouldn't I give them the best information I could about how my work might benefit them?

She's mostly interested in making the sale (not in the client's well being).

Does the value of making the sale have to conflict with the value of serving the client's wellbeing? What would need to be true for these values to support each other? And how do I know that making the sale isn't good for the client?

She's cagey about her price, and that means she's tricking people into making a commitment before they know what it will cost (and I don't want to do that).

Can I think of any reason (other than to trick someone) to delay answering a question about my fee? What if I believe that the price won't make any sense without context? If I was selling widgets by the dozen and a prospective buyer didn't know what a dozen meant, wouldn't it be more ethical to clarify that before naming the price?

She puts people on the spot (and that's mean).

Is asking people if they have a concern about the price putting them on the spot? And if so, are there times when being put on the spot serves the client? Oh! And I notice that one reason I'm afraid to ask people if they have a problem with the price is that I'm afraid the answer might be "yes," and that would mean I charge too much or that I am a crummy salesperson.

Have to Believes

One of my favorite ways of working with my negative reactions is to ask what I would have to believe in order to feel okay in a given situation. If I feel uncomfortable when clients express reservations about my fees, I ask myself, *"What would I have to believe to be okay with what I charge even when a potential client can't or won't pay that amount?"*

I don't know about you, but the first thing this question does is bring up more objections! Here's where my mind goes.

How can I be okay about this when obviously they don't trust me or think my work is worth what I am charging? And what if they really do value my work but can't afford it? How can I be okay with that?

Notice, though, I said what I would have to believe, but in reverse. One of my concerns is with trust. I can't control whether or not somebody trusts me, but I can control whether or not I am worthy of trust.

I can't control other people's financial condition, but I can question my assumption that they need something from me that they cannot afford. Can I really know that my work is the only thing standing between this person and happiness?

By looking at my fears, I discover what I would have to believe to be free from them.

From Belief to Action

It's not enough to decide what I'd have to believe to be comfortable when someone has reservations, or even objections, about my prices. If I stop here, I've just created a new story. If I don't live up to this story, it won't have a happy ending.

So I sit with my "have to believes" and ask what it would take to make them true. For example,

I would have to believe that I am trustworthy. That means living up to my commitments, keeping my promises, and telling the truth. I would have to believe that the person who hires me or buys a product can get good value from it.

What does this mean for me as an accidental entrepreneur? Among other things, it means being honest about my own financial needs. It means charging the fees I need to charge in order to reliably do good work. It means not offering discounts to get approval and then resenting the people I gave them to. It means helping clients and customers understand what I do so they can make the best decision for their own wellbeing.

Play With It

What do Russian cosmonauts, Olympic athletes, and the Green Berets have in common? They all practice for their biggest challenges by visualizing themselves performing at the peak of their abilities. When you combine visualizing yourself being effective at getting clients with the instruction, "Be Yourself," you get "Play with it."

Mind is like a frisky kitten. Give it something to play with, and watch it go! When you imagine yourself talking to a prospective client, go ahead and play with some different scenarios. You can even play with the scary ones, despite what you may have heard about the importance of positive thinking. As long as you realize that you are *playing*, you can afford to investigate all sorts of ways of being. Every variation is just another colorful ball of yarn in the kitten's paws.

Hindsight Is Foresight

One of the best ways to play with different scenarios is to replay a crummy situation. We tend to do this anyway, why not do it on purpose? When we deliberately recall a painful situation for the sake of noticing the script we were living, we can learn a whole lot. If you can read a script, you can change it.

Perhaps you're a physical therapist and you've been obsessing about not having followed up with a referral. Your neighbor said she mentioned you to her cousin, Jim, who has chronic shoulder pain, and she said you ought to call him up.

You stall. You need the work, but what are you going to say to Jim? You keep writing "call Jim" on your calendar, but you don't call. You are mad at yourself, but there it is.

To use hindsight as foresight, replay one of the times you sat at the phone not calling. Watch yourself until you have a sense of the script. In this situation, you may notice that you were running this script: *I don't want to interrupt. He doesn't want to hear form me or he would have called my office. I feel foolish. I don't want to seem like I am desperate for work.*

As best you can, just notice the script without being too hard on yourself for running it. When you have the sense of it, change position, get up and walk around the room once or twice. Then imagine that you are calling Jim. Imagine that it feels good to be phoning him. As you bring this good feeling into your body you might notice a new thought, "I'm glad to have this opportunity to be of service. I love what I do."

In your imagination, you dial the phone and get the answering machine. Imagine yourself leaving a message that comes from that thought of gratitude and service. Maybe it goes something like this:

Hello Jim. This is Adele Andersen, the physical therapist Natalie told you about. I work with a lot of folks who have chronic pain, and they are getting great results, if I do say so myself. I have some time free next Wednesday afternoon. Would you like to come by for a consultation? There'd be no charge for this. It's just an opportunity for us to connect and for you to see if my work might be right for you. My number is 123-4567.

You hang up the phone and just sit for a moment, savoring the warm feeling in your chest and throat. That felt good!

It's a Mystery

So what's the next step? It's a mystery.

You might find yourself feeling so warm and fuzzy that you actually call Jim. If you do, it will go well or it won't. Either outcome gives you more to practice with. The truth is that when we don't have a lot of clients, we might as well use our time developing the capacity to relate to them with ease.

And maybe you don't call Jim for any number of reasons. He's moved since you talked to Natalie two years ago. (!) You enjoyed the visualization and you aren't ready. It's okay. The only sensible measure of success is that you showed up for yourself and your business by paying attention, asking questions, checking in with you, and being open to what comes.

When you think about it, that's quite a lot.

Chapter 10

The Just-Right Client

I have always been an admirer. I regard the gift of admiration as indispensable if one is to amount to something; I don't know where I would be without it.
~Thomas Mann

How would it be to work with clients and customers you admire? Imagine yourself going through your day serving people that you can't help but appreciate. Nice, yes?

Not the least of the benefits of working with people we admire is that it's inspiring. Anyone who has been involved in a sport knows that we play up to the level of our competition. In business, accidental entrepreneurs live up to the level of their clientele.

When you think about it this way, it seems clear that you will do your best work and give your best talents when you consistently work with clients that fit just-right. In this chapter we'll look at how to identify the just-right client. In the next chapter, we will look at reaching them.

What Do You Want?

One surprising way to free ourselves from negative associations about business is to acknowledge the ways in which they are true for us. As human beings, we experience greed, lust, and shame as well as generosity, love, and honor. The fact that we prefer to be generous, loving, and honorable does not change that one whit.

We can experience greed without acting on it. We can be tempted to sell out without doing so. But really, who are we to pretend to be above these oh-so-human drives?

When we combine mixed motives with business, oh my! Somehow business seems to magnify our self-interest and expose it for all to see. Who do we think we are to charge so much? How can we ask clients to trust us to have their best interests at heart when we desperately need their business?

Giving in to self-protective and self-seeking motives entirely goes against our values, but in business, we can't help but notice that our motives are not entirely selfless. Is there a way out of this stalemate?

Yes. And as with so many emotional and spiritual challenges, the way out is in.

Go for What You Want

One of the hardest things for an accidental entrepreneur to do is pick a goal. We have lots of reasons for resisting goal-setting ranging from being allergic to commitment to not wanting to exclude any possibilities to not wanting to tell God what to do.

When we do set goals, we often compromise, choosing what we think is reasonable or what we think we should want. If we are lucky, we miss the mark. If we're not, we find ourselves in the embarrassing position of having what we said we wanted and feeling ungrateful and unfulfilled.

Time after time I've worked with people who spend years training to work in fields they didn't much like using skills that didn't come naturally. Without exception, these folks were very s successful in spite of the fact that they were ill-suited for their professions. But when it came to designing a business they could actually like, they balked. Here are some of the reasons they gave for not going for what they really wanted. How many of them do you recognize?

- **I could never charge that much!**
- **I'm not smart enough.** *(This from a client who had an MBA from a top school in spite of not liking business!)*
- **I'm too old.**
- **I don't want to work more than 30 hours a week while my kids are in school.**
- **I hate marketing.** *(This was said by the most outgoing and vivacious woman I've ever worked with.)*

What's wrong with this picture? How can we grow the kind of businesses we want to have if we won't acknowledge and go for what we want?

Dreams Deferred

In his excellent book, *The Power of TED* (*The Empowerment Dynamic*), David Emerald tells the story of how one man escaped the Dreaded Drama Triangle* (DDT). The DDT is the dynamic in which Victim, Persecutor, and Rescuer keep each other locked in an unproductive, stressful, and painful relationship.

At the heart of the victim role, Emerald says, is a dream deferred, something the Victim has decided is unattainable. When this dream is sufficiently important, victimhood can pervade the person's life, often to the dismay of friends and family who see how much the Victim has going for him.

Emerald proposes that the way out of the victim role is to step into the role of Creator. The Creator revives the dream. Each choice is a step toward the dream, and whether it works or not, the resulting insights move the Creator closer to his goal.

I suggest that some accidental entrepreneurs are inadvertent Victims. Having decided on some level that they cannot have

---

* Based on the Drama Triangle described by Stanley Karpman.

what they really want, every step they take is a compromise. No matter how brilliant or hard working they are, there is a sense of deprivation and loss. When we live as Victims, our strategy is to minimize pain and maximize our capacity to tolerate discomfort and disappointment.

There is a substantial risk in moving from Victim to Creator, and that is the risk of disappointment. Some part of us feels that it is better to defer the dream than to go for it and fail. That makes a certain amount of sense when we are children and our parents control the realization of our dreams. It is so frustrating to pit our desire against their superior power that we choose to give up the desire. At least then, we feel, we have taken back our right to choose.

But we are not children anymore. It's time to step out of the drama triangle and go for what we want, whether or not we think we can have it.

Application: Finding the Just-Right Client

The Three Instructions can help us with the simple-not-easy task of transforming fears about getting clients into clarity about who we serve and how.

First, let's acknowledge that, for most accidental entrepreneurs, getting clients is inseparable from earning enough money to survive, let alone thrive. You'll find more on this in Part 3, Getting Paid. For now, keep in mind that human beings are complex critters. We have mixed motives; that's Reality. Pretending that money is not a concern doesn't help us be more authentic or effective.

Then there's the problem of finding clients, let alone getting hired by them. If you aren't an old hand at getting attention, this can be daunting. Even if you do love the limelight, you may not know how to translate that into connecting with clients.

Finally, there are all the stories we tell ourselves about what clients want.

Question Stressful Thoughts

What stories do you tell yourself about getting clients? What problems do you see? Notice how you explain the difficulty of getting clients to yourself and question those explanations.

Imagine you are having the thought, "I don't want to be pushy." Take a minute to recall a situation in which you actually experienced this thought. (If you haven't been in this situation yet, imagine one.) Watch yourself in your mind's eye, and notice the way you explain the situation. Then list your thoughts.

When I invited a group to do this exercise, they came up with these explanations.

I shouldn't have to convince people to buy my work.

They ought to read the sign; it tells them everything they need to know.

It's not right that people with good personalities are better at selling.

I can't make enough money today to pay the rent, so why should I bother?

Notice that the thoughts the group came up with aren't necessarily logical. What matters is that they identified the stories they were telling themselves in the uncomfortable situation. To do that, they needed to be petty, even childish. And why not? Aren't many of our most uncomfortable thoughts petty and childish? How can we hope to question them if we won't let ourselves go?

When you have your thoughts on paper, take them to Inquiry. Working with one thought at a time, ask yourself the four questions. Write out your answers. Then find the turnarounds. See if you can find three ways in which the turnarounds are as true as your original thought.

Be Yourself

The place God calls you to is the place where your deep gladness and the world's deep hunger meet.
~Frederick Buechner

You serve best that client that fits you best. Let your mind travel to good experiences you've had working in any context, paid or volunteer. Choose one of your favorites and recall it in as much detail as possible. Notice how it felt to be working in this way. Notice your body language and mental conversation. What strengths did you contribute to this situation?

One way we know we are working with a just-right client is that they benefit not only from what we do but how we do it and who we are. It's as if the person we can't help but be blesses them (which is exactly what happens when the Channel is open). Our energy and attention are at their service, undistorted by concern with our image and self-interest.

Defining your just-right client in terms of Being Yourself may seem self-indulgent. Actually, it's the reverse. I used to be a compulsive volunteer. There are a lot of things I am good at (blush), and there's no shortage of organizations that need help. I loved riding in on my white horse and saving the day.

Of course there was the small matter of ending my commitments with burnout and resentment. And no sooner would I resign from one board or committee than I would join another. I was addicted to recognition and approval.

Confusing generosity with self-importance, I repeated the pattern in my first year of consulting, turning my clients into co-dependents. As a result, I was never satisfied with the help I provided or the progress they made.

The light went on one day during a conversation with a good friend and skillful coach, Steve Levin. I was bemoaning the fact that I didn't know what my business was about. At that time, my e-zine had 8,000 or more readers, so he quite reasonably asked me what my audience wanted from me.

I began to complain. "Most of them want marketing help," I said, "but I don't want to do that."

"Why not?" asked Steve. (I told you he was skillful.)

"Because the people who need my help are broke, needy, whiny, and unwilling to do what it takes to promote themselves."

And in that moment I finally heard myself. I was defining my clientele in terms of those least fit to use what I offered. What would happen if I focused instead on people who wanted to learn, were willing to do what it takes, and had sufficient resources to succeed? (And who the heck was I to assume that my readers were anything else?)

Duh! My perfect client was born. Not only did this new definition make me happier, it virtually guaranteed that the people who took my classes, read my work, or hired me as a coach would get what they came for.

Defining the client that fit just-right transformed my business overnight from a reasonably successful generic coaching practice to a company with an actual mission: to help people who were allergic to business succeed in self-employment.

Keep the Channel Open

If you feel depleted, overwhelmed, or frustrated, it can be hard to imagine any client as fitting just-right. Your clients need you to take care of yourself as much as you do.

Think about what allowed you to show up at your best in various situations. What foods make you feel energetic without being riled up? What spiritual practices help you to do your best and let go of the results? When you look at what it really takes for you to give your best, make sure you include that as business overhead. It may not be tax deductible (check with your accountant), but one way or another you need to charge enough to pay for yoga classes, retreat time, and whatever else feeds you.

Who Has Time for This?

If you need clients now, you may wonder if you have time to question your thoughts, meditate on good experiences, and work on getting to know your just-right client—all before you start promoting yourself. If that's so, ask yourself if you can afford *not* to do this work.

The Way of the Accidental Entrepreneur is what Jack Kornfeld calls a path of heart. It's a journey toward what Abraham Maslow called self-actualization and Carl Jung referred to as individuation. The stakes are high, and they have to be. A journey toward anything less than self-awareness and service is simply not worth making.

The question is not, "Is it possible to grow a successful business that fits just-right?" The question is, "Is it possible for an accidental entrepreneur to truly succeed in a business that *doesn't* fit?"

Time and again I have seen artists, coaches, and other self-employed folks from financial planners to building contractors mired in businesses that almost fit. They earn enough to get by, but never enough to rejoice. Occasionally they get a client or customer that they adore working with. Mostly they feel vaguely resentful about having to market their work to people who don't get it.

It doesn't have to be this way. It doesn't take any longer to build a business that fits just-right than to cobble together one that pinches and pulls at you. Both take a tremendous amount of time and energy. That's the way it is. The only question is whether you'll spend that energy trying to turn yourself into something you aren't or figuring out how to use your strengths to do what needs to be done.

The just-right customer and client, by definition, want what you have to offer. Anything that keeps you from a free and easy exchange of information and value with your just-right customers will cost you a lot more time and money than following the Three Instructions. Ask me: For eight years in Mollycoddles I believed my unquestioned thoughts about customers. I don't regret that for it brought me to this place; it was a great education. I do hope I can save you at least some of the time and frustration I experienced.

Self-Esteem and Your Clients

Your just-right customer deserves service whether or not you happen to be operating at the peak of self-esteem.

Just as a friend may rightfully resent being pushed away when you feel "less than," your just-right customers are ill-served when you withdraw just because your self-esteem has bottomed out.

It's natural to retreat when you feel low or inadequate, but it's unfair to do it to a customer. How can you make good on your offers if you're hiding out with your old bad self, replaying your most embarrassing moments and screening action features based on your greatest fears?

You may feel that hiding out is more ethical than promoting your work when you are full of self-doubt—but can you be sure? Is holding back for fear of being less than perfect really an act of integrity and service?

When you place your self-esteem between you and a customer, you're like a teenager that leaves her date out in the cold while she agonizes over a blemish. A customer deserves a business relationship grounded in reality, not in the equivalent of a Harlequin romance.

If you're serious about growing your business, find ways to show up as you really are. For tips on how to do this (because, after all, there is a difference between what is appropriate in business and friendship), read on.

They Want You

Be who you are and say what you feel cause people who mind don't matter, and people who matter don't mind.
~Dr. Seuss

Your personality is an important part of what differentiates you from other businesses offering similar products and services. Are you a funny, organized, motherly midwife? Or a charming, blunt career coach? It's almost certain that lots of people do what you do and do it as well or better. However, it is highly unlikely that anyone else does it quite like you do. Make it easy for people to tell how well you're likely to fit.

Praise

It's not always easy to receive praise, yet doing so is an important part of keeping the channel open.

1. Write down, word for word, the praise you received.

2. Read what you have written three times out loud. After each reading, jot down three praiseworthy things about yourself.

3. Buy some stickers and put them up around your home and office. These will be a visual reminder to open yourself in a detached and compassionate manner to the positive things people say about you and to the possibility that they are TRUE.

4. Make a daily intention to hear more clearly what people see in you and to use your talents and abilities in a joyous and easy way to serve your purpose in this life.

5. Notice when you fantasize about bad things that might result from thinking well of yourself. Write them down and take them to Inquiry.

The common idea that success spoils people by making them vain, egotistic, and self-complacent is erroneous. On the contrary, it makes them, for the most part, humble, tolerant, and kind. Failure makes people bitter and cruel. ~Somerset Maugham

Chapter 11

Courting Business

My good friend, Marsh Terry, wrote a workbook on marketing as well as a newspaper column called *Courting Business*. In the ten or so years since he first gave me the book, I haven't found a better metaphor for the way accidental entrepreneurs are designed to get clients and customers.

Some business-building systems are more like speed-dating than courting. Put out the equivalent of five minutes worth of seductive conversation and hope for some action.

Courting business takes time, respect, and persistence. Oh, and a spark of romance.

More than 25 years ago, a copier salesman came to my husband's business. At the time, I was the self-appointed business manager, so I got the pitch. He sized up the office quickly (and respectfully). His questions opened my eyes about what we needed. Jaded as I was about salespeople, he simply couldn't make a wrong move. To this day I feel privileged to have bought a copier from that guy.

What is it that made buying a copy machine into a peak experience? Caring and expertise, for starters. Enthusiasm. Availability. Honesty, of course. These add up to conviction about the right solution for the customer and the willingness to walk away without the business if it's not the right fit.

The paradox is that in order to get clients you have to let go of looking for them. When we look for clients, people know we have an ulterior motive. They can sense neediness. A conversation that might have been mutually enjoyable becomes a game of dodge-em. You do your best to talk about your work (or not), and the other person does their best to seem interested (or not) without getting roped in.

Those parenthetical "or nots" show that the game takes place within each party as well as between them. That doesn't leave a lot of bandwidth for authentic connection.

But thanks to the soullessness of mass marketing, we have come to believe that business happens in spite of relationships, not because of them. This may explain how perfectly lovely people find themselves mumbling stilted, pre-mixed elevator speeches at networking events instead of actually connecting to the people they meet.

Of course, it is difficult to have a spontaneous conversation about your work when you are not clear about what you do, not only from your point of view, but also from the point of view of a customer. This exercise will help you.

Exercise: What Do You Do?

If you ask me what I came to do in this world, I, an artist, I will answer you: I am here to live out loud.
~Emile Zola

Find a quiet spot where you can work undisturbed for at least 30 minutes. Relax your belly and take a few full, easy breaths. Notice the sensations of support wherever your body rests on a surface. Relax into this support.

When you are ready, invite into your awareness aspects of your work that amaze and delight you. Jot down words and short phrases as they occur to you. Don't worry about making sense.

When you feel complete, look at what you have written and select two words that really capture what you love about your work. Trust yourself and go with your instincts. There are no wrong choices.

Look up each word in both a dictionary and thesaurus. Copy the definitions word for word, even if they don't seem relevant. Do the same for the synonyms. To go deeper, look up the roots of your words in an etymological dictionary. Google "Indo-European roots" to find online references.

Read what you've copied out loud. Let yourself muse about the words and their definitions. Jot down any associations that show up.

Make a clean copy of your work and keep it where you will see it often. Review it before you write or speak about your work. Play with using words from your list when you tell others what you do.

Playing Hide and Seek or "I can be whatever you want me to be. Go away, I hate you!"

It's ironic that accidental entrepreneurs, who by and large place a high value on authenticity, often stop being themselves when they start reaching out to clients. Perhaps it's because we think of business as something alien to our values. We reject what we feel is false or dehumanizing, then we unconsciously adapt our behavior to what we have rejected. We become what we hate.

Case Study: I Can Do Anything

All my life, I always wanted to be somebody. Now I see that I should have been more specific. ~Jane Wagner

One of my clients learned this the hard way, investing months of her creative time and hard-earned resources in making custom clothing. Project after project fell short of the mark, surprising and disappointing her clients and leaving her broke, embarrassed, and frustrated. She had tried her best to match her talents with the desires of the marketplace and failed, or so she thought.

On reflection she realized that she had not really matched her talents to the market at all. A brilliant colorist, designer, and innovator, she had tried to fill a niche that required the skills of a translator, fitter, and cheerleader. Perhaps she could have succeeded with a partner who brought complementary skills to the business, but alone, she worked herself into debt and frustration.

Fortunately, this same designer started saying "No" to inappropriate projects. She built new working arrangements and products around her strengths. She hired an employee to handle the things she was not good at. She followed up with every customer to find out what worked and what didn't. The testimonials about what worked attracted more just-right clients. The information about what didn't work showed her what to improve or what not to do at all.

It is important to look to the market to see what prospective customers and clients want. But look for how the needs and desires of the market match your strengths, talents, and passions. Say no to the opportunities that are a poor match so that your vision and your resources can be focused on the projects and relationships that are most likely to succeed.

The Power of One

One complaint about business is that it is impersonal, even inconsiderate. Back when Bell Telephone ("Ma Bell") had a monopoly on telephone service in the USA, people joked that their tagline should be: "We don't care. We don't have to."

The accidental entrepreneur wants clients she can relate to, not faceless entities. "Every client is an individual," she insists, when I ask her to profile her just-right client. And she's right.

Inexperienced speakers have trouble making eye contact with their audiences. How do you make eye contact with 400 people? Speaking coaches have the answer: One pair of eyes at a time. When a speaker pauses to make eye contact with one individual and then another, everyone in the audience experiences a vicarious sense of connection.

The same thing happens when you communicate with prospective clients. Whether you are blogging, writing an article, or creating a brochure, the way to connect with your just-right client is to talk to one specific person.

Finding Ellie

Ellie is the name I gave the prototypical accidental entrepreneur, the just-right client for this book.

Here's how I describe her:

- 40-something, has two teenage kids, a single mom.
- Has been self-employed for a few years. She gets by, but barely.
- Owns her home and has a hefty mortgage.
- Has more credit card debt than she would like, but she also has a good credit record.
- Has lots of interests. Would rather learn something new than keep doing the same thing over and over.
- Likes her work, at least she thought she did. These days she wonders.
- Spends a fair amount of time putting out fires (complaints, rush projects, fixing mistakes).
- She blames herself when things go wrong.
- Sometimes she escapes into novels or crossword puzzles.
- She is afraid to narrow her focus for fear of losing business.
- She wants to raise her rates, but she can't see how she can when she isn't meeting her own standards for good work. How can she charge more unless she improves her service? How can she improve her service when she can't keep up as it is?
- She sometimes feels like hiding from her clients.

You may not be exactly like Ellie, though I'm willing to bet that a lot of those characteristics resonate. The details may vary, but the fundamentals probably click—otherwise you wouldn't be reading this.

Your job now is to get to know your just-right client as well as I know Ellie.

Give Your Clients What They Want

Be up front, even bold, in stating how what you do makes things better for them so that they can make a decision about whether to ask for more information. This respects their time and attention by answering the question, "What can you do for me?"

Understand what it takes for you to deliver consistent value. How much time? How much money? How much energy? What kind of commitment? What support? What resources? What else?

When you know what you need in order to come through for your customers, set your prices, policies, and procedures accordingly and make it easy for your customers to understand them.

Chapter 12

Selling to Your Just-Right Client

I s there anything more painful than selling? Probably. Still, I was in business for eighteen years before I realized that selling is an integral part of the client relationship. To not sell is to abandon the members of your audience who want more from you. It's like keeping them forever suspended in "first-date" mode.

Speaking of Pain

The first duty of sales is to talk about pain. Clients need us to speak to their pain. Clients have over 3,000 other messages coming at them every day—and that's in addition to the 50,000 or so messages in their internal dialogues.

Human beings can only process about 300 messages in a day, which means that 2700 messages are going to be ignored. Pain is the quick-sort mechanism we use to decide what gets through.

We may like good news, but it is pain that grabs our attention. Given the deluge of information in contemporary life, good news rarely penetrates the awareness of a person who is not predisposed to pay attention.

Does this apply even when the good news pertains directly to what your client cares for most?

Absolutely.

People who care deeply about something, their horses, for example, immerse themselves in horse information and resources.

The more experienced they are, the more information they are likely to have. Whether or not it is good information is another matter entirely, and one that does not change the fact that horse-lovers are already getting bombarded with messages about horses.

Your prospective client simply does not have the bandwidth to notice the solutions you offer when they are already getting plenty of data from sources they know and trust.

Unless you address what hurts.

This is why, even when the problem you will solve is structural or systemic, you must talk to your customers in terms of symptoms. Knowing the problem is not enough. You must know and be able to articulate the problem in terms of your client's painful experience.

Different people with different values and concerns will experience identical problems differently. The rider who competes in dressage will have different priorities than the breeder of thoroughbreds, and they may make very different decisions about how to train and care for their animals. When you understand this principle you will begin to understand why the more narrowly you define the community that you serve, the more successful your marketing will be.

Now we can begin at the beginning, defining your market. Having established that symptomatic pain is the pivotal element in reaching your market, you will determine just who that market is.

Exercise: What Do You Want for Your Clients?

What do you want to give to your just-right client? What expectations would you like them to have?

Remember, by definition, your just-right client is someone who will surely benefit from working with you. You don't have to persuade them to buy something they don't want. Working in your notebook, make a list of the specific, measurable things you want to deliver to your just-right client.

Here's what a client of mine wrote about what she wants writers who hire her as an editor to get from working with her.

1. Peace of mind; confidence that their manuscript is error-free
2. Useful insights into content, structure, flow, and wording
3. Challenges to their ideas
4. Focus on their inner truth
5. A refined vision
6. Ability to get past stumbling points in their writing process
7. Information about publishing in creative ways
8. Pleasant and fun working experience
9. Openness, honor, and respect
10. Appreciation for them and their efforts
11. Availability, access when they need me
12. A helpful website and newsletter
13. A model of being positive and grounded
14. Work from a spiritual foundation
15. Personal service
16. A complete job
17. Extra value
18. Good value for the fee
19. Maintain professionalism and professional growth
20. Serve them from the vision of my perfect business

This list captures what this editor truly wants to deliver. When she imagines delivering this, she feels proud and enthusiastic about her work. She can readily see why her just-right client would hire her.

And she can see that delivering all of that without support would be almost impossible. At best, she'd come through for a few clients before falling prey to burn out. At worst, she'd be so daunted by the scope of her offer that she would compromise on the fly, depriving herself of the opportunity to do great work and her clients of the opportunity to benefit from it.

That's why the next step was to figure out what it would take for her to follow through.

What Do You Need to Do Your Best Work?

When we want good things for our clients, it's easy to worry about falling short of the mark. The more we think about what it would be like to disappoint our clients, the more we shrink back from authentic connection. In no time at all, our sincere aspiration to serve is replaced by paralysis.

The remedy is to recognize that we can't create something from nothing. If we plan to deliver value to our clients, we need to build in sources of energy and support.

Review the list of what you want to deliver to your just-right client. In your notebook, write down everything you can think of that you would need to reliably follow through.

In the case of the editor, she quickly realized that maintaining a helpful website and newsletter, being available, providing extra value, and staying in touch with her clients—to name just a few items—would require considerable time and money.

In addition, the personal and professional attributes she wants to bring to her work have to be supported. It takes time, money, energy, resources to take additional training, to spend time in prayer and meditation, to exercise, to read, to regularly connect with her vision, and to get help from others.

So, when she chooses for her just-right customer to expect to pay a fair and reliable fee, that fee has to be adequate to meet all those expenses.

Low-balling or quoting the smallest possible fee will put a crimp in the creative conduit you are, resulting in lower value to your clients (and a loss of pride in your work).

Whatever you want for your clients, your fees need to support what it takes to deliver that. Any less and you make it impossible for you to live up to what the expectations you want your clients to have.

What if Nothing Happens?

So you've taken action, and nothing is happening. What's up with that? You probably have a dozen explanations, and I bet none of them are positive.

The thing is, no matter how much of an impression you make when you reach out, folks are sailing their own ships. Here's an excerpt from an exchange with a client, Suzie, about the thought, "None of my contacts have gotten back with me yet."

None of your contacts have gotten back with you yet. Is it true?

In this case, it is factually true that they have not gotten back with you yet. However, it is never Reality that hurts; it's our thoughts about Reality. So, when the stressful thought is patently true, it can be useful to expand it: "None of my contacts have gotten back with me yet, and it means that..."

Then you can do The Work on your thoughts about what it means. Of course, you can also stay with the first thought, and answer question one, "Yes, it is true." Just keep working through the questions.

Can you absolutely know that it is true?

If yes, fine. If no, fine. In either case, just answer the question and move to question 3.

How do you react when you believe that thought? What happens?

This is the juicy place. Where do you go in your mind when you think the thought, "None of my contacts have gotten back with me yet"? How do you treat them (in your mind)? How do you treat your family? How do you treat yourself? Whose business are you in?

Who would you be without the thought?

In this moment, who would you be without the thought, "None of my contacts have gotten back with me yet"?

Thinking back to the time when the thought was discouraging, who would you have been in that moment without the thought?

Here is where Suzie went with her Inquiry:

My contacts haven't gotten back to me and that means... they decided they weren't interested in my book after all.

Is it true? *I rather doubt it. It's good, and it's a celebration of something important to them.*

Can I absolutely know that it is true? *No way. To even assume so is to be about their business rather than mine.*

How do I react when I believe that thought? What happens? *I feel like a second-rate writer, like a goofball who asked for attention without having anything of real substance to offer. I treat them as the cool people who have better things to do than mess with me. I treat my husband as the confident-engine-of-prosperity-dragging along this flawed-and-delusional-would-be-writer half of our marriage.*

Who would I be without this thought? *A writer with a noteworthy and well-written novel that is gathering momentum.*

Turnarounds

They have gotten back to me. *It's entirely possible that my contacts are brimming with ideas upon perusing my book, which they want to sort out before getting back to me. Maybe they're even networking amongst themselves.*

I haven't gotten back to my contacts. *This is true—maybe truer. I'm the one that stands to gain here; it's my job to follow up.*

I haven't gotten back to me. *Yes. I am in their business, which leaves me feeling abandoned and hopeless. I need to get back to me by re-connecting with my purpose for writing the book and giving me the benefit of brainstorming ways to promote it.*

When Prospects Tune Out

If you've ever come upon a deer in the roadway while driving at night, you've seen a deer freeze. Though tragically unsuccessful on today's roads, freezing is a highly effective survival strategy in the deer's native habitat.

That's because, in the backwoods, a flash of light is often moonlight reflecting off the eyes of a predator. The deer stands perfectly still to avoid detection and capture.

Tuning out is the new way to freeze

Like many people, you've probably learned to tune out the constant barrage of advertising that assaults us 24/7. For the contemporary consumer (don't you hate that word?), tuning out is a strategy for evading "capture."

But why would anyone tune you out?

You're a nice person. You don't especially like marketing. You certainly don't view your prospective clients or customers as "consumers." But when you deliver your hard-earned elevator speech, you can see people's eyes glaze over as they tune out. What's up with that?

They've heard it all before. Your product or service can be utterly unique and perfectly suited to a customer's needs, but your elevator speech sounds tediously familiar. Here's why.

Your customers' eyes and ears have become accustomed to mass-market advertising. Even if what you say is unique, glib phrases, canned elevator speeches, and being too cute or clever makes your message sound about as relevant as a bicycle to a fish.

I'm not saying that connecting with folks before you speak to them will make them hire you or buy your products. What it will do is establish you as a real person in a real conversation. It will keep folks from tuning you out before they can discover if you have anything to offer.

How Selling Builds Trust

Trust is built when two or more parties make and fulfill commitments with each other. We build trust with clients and customers when we offer something of value and ask for payment, then live up to our end of the bargain.

Does the idea of coming right out and selling to your customers give you the heebie-jeebies? It did me. I'm fine with marketing, but selling? Yikes!

For eight of the nine years that I wrote my newsletter, the content was more than 90% editorial. In that period, there were less than a handful of times that I sent an email to my list that wasn't content-focused.

In 2006, I started sending emails to promote (and sell) the Authentic Wealth Tele-retreat. These were strictly about the program with no other content. I got some pushback from friends and others who like the newsletter but aren't actually in the market for my services. A couple of people who might be prospective clients also complained. But are they really right for me if deleting an occasional email is too much trouble to take in return for a free publication full of wonderful useful information they've been enjoying for years ☺?

More to the point, 14 people unsubscribed from my list during the first three months that I sent sales emails. That's 0.14% of my readers. In the past, I would have shriveled up with shame about the people who left the list (and who, for all I know, were simply changing email addresses). And how well do you think it serves the other 99.86% of the list when I do that?

Until I decided to sell to the people on my list, life at Shaboom was part dream, part nightmare, a rollercoaster of excitement and depletion. My energy would go up when people praised me and down when they didn't. I lived in fear of offending my audience.

That's no way to build a long-term relationship, let alone a thriving community.

When we avoid selling to people, we keep customers at arms length, turning them into strangers. Our businesses cannot survive on the kindness of strangers. (And why should strangers take care of us, anyway?)

Enough. It's the upside to this story that I am itching to share, so here's the good news. When we sell to our customers, everything changes.

Beyond the Sale

When you sell and a customer buys, the whole world changes. Does the customer love what they bought? Wonderful! Find out how else you can help, and sell them something else. Not to milk them, not to take advantage of them, but to help. (That is why you're in business, isn't it?)

Is your customer dissatisfied? Excellent! Find out why. Ask how you can improve the product or service, and, provided that the customer fits your business "just-right," they'll tell you exactly what you need to do to make them happy and to attract more people just like them.

More customers mean more people taking ownership, and that is the basis for a community. Yes, there's more to growing a community than this, but you won't have one to grow until you start selling.

Why Nice People Don't Sell

Your task is not to seek for love, but merely to seek and find all the barriers within yourself that you have built against it. ~Jelaluddin Rumi

I don't know about you, but here's why I resist selling. I want to be liked. Okay, you may be more evolved than I am. But consider these classic reasons for avoiding anything that resembles selling.

- You don't want to seem pushy. (You want to be liked.)

- You are afraid your work isn't good enough. (You are afraid a customer might be disappointed and then they won't like you.)
- You can't stand rejection. (What is rejection except the belief that the person who is saying "no" doesn't like you?)

If you have read this far, odds are very high that you, like me, place a very high value on being liked. There is nothing wrong with that. But are you willing to let the desire to be liked prevent people from benefiting from your work? Are you willing to place being liked ahead of creating revenue streams that will energize your business and help you generate quality products and services on an ongoing basis?

Smile. Your Customers Love You.

Here's the part that will make you smile big time. Imagine having plenty of bandwidth to take care of your customers. Imagine being comfortable in your own skin, satisfied to be doing your best for your just-right customers. (Goodbye, perfectionism!) Imagine looking forward to feedback, both positive and negative, from customers that are part of a growing community.

That's what selling to people can do.

Chapter 13
Trouble at the Border

*H*ealthy boundaries are essential for a healthy business. That sounds right, but what does it mean?

First, let's make a distinction between defensive and defining boundaries. When we are in unfamiliar territory, we tend to set defensive boundaries. In business this can look like micro-managing our client relationships and expecting our clients to remember our every preference.

I've done this, by the way, so I know of what I speak. Early in my coaching career I decided that I would only coach on certain days. I told clients what days I was working and asked them not to call at other times. I fully expected them to honor my calendar, as if they had nothing else to think about.

Naturally, some clients called on my off days. After all, it was a business phone. Usually I'd pick up and lecture them about respecting my stated days and hours. What was I thinking?

I felt besieged, trapped in the fortress of my office cum art studio. It sounds silly, but it was dreadfully serious at the time.*

---

*Actually, I have a better – and more embarrassing – example. For a time, my art-to-wear studio, Mollycoddles, was located on the second floor of a tiny mall. The upstairs got hardly any traffic, but as soon as I hung out a sign saying "Artist at work. Please do not disturb," people seemed to come out of the woodwork. Could I suggest a good place to eat? Where might they find a public restroom? It drove me crazy. Gee, why do you suppose I never succeeded in retail?

That sort of boundary leaves no room to move. There is barely room to breathe. After a while, we get impatient, cranky, and resentful. Maybe dealing with people is just too hard.

When we focus on defense, we invite offense. The harder we try to enforce defensive boundaries, the more boundary violations we experience. The problem is that while defensive boundaries usually fail at keeping craziness at bay, they often succeed at keeping business from getting in.

Avoiding Boundaries

At the other extreme, we may avoid setting boundaries or set them too loosely, trying to make sure we don't offend a current or potential client. We may say yes when we mean no or waffle on our prices or terms. Sometimes we don't set any boundaries at all until we burn out or feel so taken advantage of that we retreat or strike back.

When we avoid setting boundaries our business turns into a cave, a tight, dark space we back into when we are under siege. We end up alone, cramped, and hungry. This is not what we had in mind when we went to work for ourselves.

Defining Boundaries

Fortunately, there is a better way. We can use boundaries to define our business rather than defend ourselves. Defining boundaries are not solid, impermeable walls designed to keep invaders out but open, flexible structures that give context to our interactions and shape expectations.

These are like the fences you see around a pasture or playground. They define limits without stifling life. They admit light and air; they allow us to see out and others to see in.

Working within boundaries like this is liberating. There is room to move, explore, and experiment. We know where our business ends and our customers' business begins. We can see who is approaching and choose how to respond.

Maintaining defining boundaries feels good, like walking a fence line. We oil the latches on the gates, replace broken posts, and trim the hedges—taking care of the boundary that helps everything feel orderly and safe.

Practice: Questioning Scary Thoughts About Clients

From time to time we all have scary thoughts about clients. Let some of your scary thoughts about clients pop into your mind right now. (They probably showed up as soon as I mentioned them.) Make a list of as many scary thoughts about clients as you can think of. Include all of them: the silly ones, the embarrassing ones, and the ones that seem true.

Example: Fear of Not Meeting Expectations

I'm afraid that, if I get clients, I won't be able to live up to their expectations.

I'm afraid they won't want to pay me after I've done the work.

I won't have the focus to complete the project on time. If I get clients, I won't have time for my grandkids. My colleagues will be jealous and judgmental.

I'll have to wear a suit and go to social events I don't enjoy, I won't be able to be myself.

Choose one thought that is especially uncomfortable. Do The Work on it. See if you can find three examples of how every turnaround is as true or truer than your original thoughts.

The Myth of Fear as Motivator

Some folks don't want to let go of their scary thoughts for fear that, if they do, they won't take any action at all. They imagine that fear is a good motivator.

But what really happens when you focus on your scary thoughts about clients? Whatever your fears motivate you to do is only about alleviating your anxiety. The action you take depends on what you fear the most.

This has a couple of serious consequences. For one, as soon as your anxiety is alleviated, you stop doing whatever you were doing that helped. For another, the only actions available to you are the ones you can imagine from within your framework of fear. Finally, when you're motivated by fear, every action is about self-protection, not service.

Given all that, it's no surprise that our efforts to get clients backfire when they are based on fear. We aren't thinking about how we might serve prospective clients so much as how we can reduce our own anxiety. While we may feel like shy wallflowers, we can come across as sleazy losers or hucksters on the make. Ouch! Why would anyone that we want to work with respond to that? (Yes, I exaggerate. And yet people can almost smell fear. It isn't attractive.)

Knowing that fear is a crummy motivator won't make fear go away. However, when you stop using your fears to spur you into action, you can start using them productively.

Productive Fear

When we distill fear to its essence, we discover that it always signals the possible loss of something we have or want. When fear sends the signal that we stand to lose something we care about, it is also pointing to something we very much need to know: what we want and what we care about.

Fear, in and of itself, is no more informative than the ring of a phone. The ring of a phone tells you someone (or something, in the case of auto-dialers and pre-recorded messages) wants your attention. Until you answer the phone, you cannot know for certain how much of your attention the call deserves or what you might gain in return.

In other words, when a phone rings, you make a decision to answer it or not. Maybe you check the caller ID to see if you recognize who is calling. Maybe you glance at your watch to see if this is a call you were expecting. One way or another, you gather information—often subconsciously, before you decide to answer.

When fear rings our chimes, we tend to take the call automatically. Without even thinking, we decide how to respond. We take fear in stride if it is related to something around which we have a lot of confidence, the way an experienced actor may relate to stage-fright or a skilled cyclist approach a race.

But when we experience fear of the unknown, especially something outside of our social context, we assume the worst.* We interpret a signal (something you care about could be at risk) as a fact (you will almost certainly lose something important to you).

When we work for ourselves, fear that we won't attract clients is a signal that our self-respect, material wellbeing, and social standing are at risk. That is true. But to say that those things (and others that are equally important) are at risk is not the same as saying we have to lose them.

In fact, when we learn to work with it, fear can show us exactly what we need to know in order to create businesses that fit just-right. It can show us what we really want.

Contemplating what you want (instead of obsessing about what you are afraid you can't have) makes planning natural (and fun). This is especially true when you unhook wanting from getting. When you want what you want and let go of the results, performance anxiety turns into anticipation. There's no telling what might happen next.

---

* Some people, me for example, are counter-phobic. We may respond to fear of the unknown by ignoring it, denying it, or forging ahead. When this works, it's fine, but in the case of the unknown, it can mean we act without sufficient preparation. That can lead to failure and discouragement.

Application: Productive Fear

When we're afraid, it's natural to want to be anywhere but in our own skin, anyone but who we really are. Mostly, we want not to be afraid. The thing is, we are afraid. The first step to transforming paralyzing fear into productive fear is to accept this and make room for it. In other words, be yourself, be *with* yourself, as you experience fear.

We make room for fear by stopping for a minute and noticing what it feels like in our body. As we become aware of resisting the experience of fear, we can experiment with making room for the experience instead. Don't worry if this doesn't exactly make sense. Just close your eyes and let your body show you what needs to happen. You can even ask your body to do just that.

Keep the Channel Open

When we are afraid, we may shut off connection with Source. Of course, this isn't our intention. But when we argue with our real feelings or are afraid there is something wrong with us, the channel gets pretty constricted. To open the channel, ask yourself what would have to be true for you to feel safe from your fear.

Choose one of the fears from your list of scary thoughts about clients. (See Questioning Scary Thoughts About Clients, page 120.) For now, choose one fear for the sake of walking through the exercise. Later, you can repeat this process with as many of your fears as you like.

Write the fear at the top of a sheet in your notebook. Below it, write the following question.

What would have to be true for me to feel safe from this fear?

Example

I'm afraid that, if I get clients, I won't be able to live up to their expectation.

What would have to be true for me to feel safe from this fear?

My clients trust me. I can deliver what they expect They made a good choice when they hired me. I know what I am doing. I know I will follow through.

Now it's your turn. Open your notebook and write down what you would need to believe in order to be safe from your fear. When you are finished, take a few minutes to notice how you are feeling. What's going on in your body? What emotions are showing up? What automatic thoughts do you have? Make a few notes about what you observe.

Question Stressful Thoughts

Take each of your answers to Inquiry. Remember to simplify your answers if necessary so that you are questioning one thought at a time. For example, if you answered the question, "What would need to be true for me to be safe from this fear?" by saying, "My clients trust me," you could question the thought, **My clients need to trust me.**

Similarly, if you answered the question, "What would need to be true for me to be safe?" by saying, "They made a good choice when they hired me," you could question the thought, **I need to know that they make a good choice when they hire me.**

If you need help framing a statement to take to Inquiry, ask your support team or post a request in Shaboom County.

The Willing Suspension of Disbelief

Letting go of fear sometimes requires what Samuel Taylor Coleridge called a willing suspension of disbelief. When you read a poem or a novel, you realize you are not dealing with facts. You willingly suspend disbelief so that the images, characters, and events come alive in your imagination as if they were real.

In the same way, you can willingly suspend disbelief so that you can imagine how it would be to feel safe and secure in your dealings with clients. This way you can experiment with different thoughts and scenarios, playing with possible ways to be with clients.

Suspending disbelief can sound like a gimmick for replacing your scary thoughts about clients with a made-up story. The story may feel good in the short run, but what difference does that make if you end up with the same reality, one where clients are hard to find?

Doubt is tremendously important. Without the capacity to doubt, we can't test the validity of what others tell us, not to mention our own perceptions. Without doubt, we are innocents lost in a dangerous world.

But there is a big difference between the kind of doubt that exists to point out a need to validate information and the kind of doubt that is a habit.

When we are outside of our comfort zones, doubt can become a habit. We doubt reflexively to protect ourselves from embarrassment and disappointment. We use doubt to keep us from stepping outside the limits of certainty.

That's perfectly fine if you want to stay where you are. But if you want something other than what you have right now, you need to venture beyond what you already know. You need to take informed risks. The willing suspension of disbelief recognizes that doubt exists and sets it aside so you can explore possibilities.

Chapter 14

Judge Your Clients as Yourself

Compassion automatically invites you to relate with people because you no longer regard people as a drain on your energy. ~Chogyam Trungpa

A funny thing happens when we have stressful thoughts about clients: we tend to judge ourselves.

As children we were taught that it's not nice to judge others. And if you've done much work on yourself, you've probably discovered that the flaws you see in others can generally be found in you as well.

So it is natural to look first at our own faults when we experience conflict or stress with clients. It's natural, but it isn't necessarily honest or fruitful. In fact, judging yourself can actually get in the way of resolving fear and stress.

Concept Versus Experience

I am a man; nothing human is alien to me. ~Publius Terence

We can know conceptually that our judgments of others are projections, yet we experience those judgments as true. We can deny our experience all day long, but experience will always win out over concepts.

When we turn judgments about others against ourselves, we end up fighting Reality on two fronts. The stressful thought we are experiencing is one front. Denying our experience is the other.

It's a no-win situation.

The harder we try to rise above our judgments, the more deeply entrenched they become. And often we end up treating others as poorly as we are treating ourselves.

This can be heartbreaking on so many levels. But there is a way out.

Judge Your Clients Early and Often

> *The remarkable thing is that we really love our neighbor as ourselves: we do unto others as we do unto ourselves. We hate others when we hate ourselves. We are tolerant toward others when we tolerate ourselves. We forgive others when we forgive ourselves. We are prone to sacrifice others when we are ready to sacrifice ourselves.*
> *~Eric Hoffer*

Every stressful thought about clients—getting them, keeping them, working with them, losing them—is an invitation to awakening. Far from being a sly way to trash people, judging them and then bringing your judgments to Inquiry is the short cut to authentic, appreciative relationship.

A great way to capture your judgments before you can deny them is to stalk your moods. Track them like a hunter. When you catch the scent of resentment, irritation, or sadness, look for someone to blame. Judge them on paper, ask four questions, and turn it around.

The worst thing that can happen is that you will start looking forward to feeling judgmental. That may sound nuts right now, but when you experience the freedom that flows from following the simple directions of The Work, you will understand.

Example: Judging a Client Who Cancels*

Here's a worksheet a client wrote when one of her own clients canceled a session just an hour or so before it was scheduled to take place. Notice how she kept it simple, using short, clear sentences. The pettier and simpler you can be on your Judge Your Neighbor worksheets, the better!

1. I'm angry at Xaviera because she canceled our appointment at the last minute.

2. I need Xaviera to respect my time. I need her to cancel appointments at least 24 hours in advance.

3. She should offer to pay for the appointment.

4. Xaviera is self-centered, inconsiderate, and unconscious about money.

5. I'm afraid that if I ask her to pay for the missed appointment she will stop coming to see me altogether. I'm afraid that I can't be happy in my business.

Now it's your turn. Complete the Judge Your Client Worksheet on the following page. If you need a refresher (and even if you don't), there are detailed instructions in Chapter 5. For more information, including a pamphlet that explains in detail how to do The Work, go to www.thework.com.

---

*From the Mini Worksheet, © 2002, Byron Katie, Inc. To learn more about The Work, read *Loving What Is* and visit www.thework.org.

Judge Your Client Worksheet*

Fill in the worksheet using simple statements. Keep it simple, and don't be evolved. The pettier you can let yourself be, the more freedom you will experience in The Work.

1. I'm upset, angry, or sad at _____

because_____

_____

_____

2. I need _____

to _____

_____

_____

3. _____

should_____

_____

_____

4. _____

is _____

_____

_____

_____

* Adapted from the Judge Your Neighbor Worksheet, copyright Byron Katie International. For more information about The Work and to purchase a copy of *Loving What Is* (the primary "how to"), visit www.thework.com.

After Writing a Worksheet

When your worksheet is complete, read through it from top to bottom. Ideally, you will do this with a partner or your study group. When your worksheet feels complete, take each stressful thought or concept to The Work.

When a Stressful Thought Is True

What do you do if your stressful thought is true? If Xaviera really did cancel right before an appointment, it might seem silly to question it.

Here are two ways you can proceed when dealing with a stressful fact.

1. See what happens when you apply the four questions and turnarounds to the original statement. Say "yes" to the first two questions. When you get to question three, *How do you react when you think that thought? What happens?*, pay particular attention to where your mind travels when you think the thought. Do you find yourself imagining how inconsiderate Xaviera was? Does this lead you to think about how little she respects you? Take these underlying thoughts to Inquiry.

2. You can achieve similar results by asking why the factual thought is stressful. What does it mean that Xaviera canceled? Write down your stressful thought and follow it with "it means that…" Make a list of all the things the thought means. Question the thoughts on your list.

When my client did this about Xaviera's cancellation, she came up with this list.

- She doesn't respect my time.
- She is unprofessional.
- She is irresponsible.
- She is taking advantage of me.
- She is dishonest.

What to Do With Your Answer to Number Four

The fourth item on the Judge Your Client worksheet is your chance to say what you think of the person you are judging. My client wrote, "Xaviera is self-centered, inconsiderate, and unconscious about money."

Sometimes you will find that, having questioned your first three answers, you don't really believe your thought anymore. In this case, you can go directly to the turnaround, applying each of the traits you listed about the other person to yourself. "I am self-centered, inconsiderate, and unconscious about money."

Take the traits one at a time and see if you can find three concrete examples of how they are as true or truer about you. Here's what my client found.

> **I am self-centered.** *This is at least as true. I am only concerned about how this affects me. I haven't even tried to see this from Xaviera's point of view.*

> **I am inconsiderate.** *This is at least as true. I haven't considered what Xaviera may be dealing with. I haven't asked myself what she may need in this situation.*

When it came to the turnaround, "I am unconscious about money," my client felt stuck. How could this apply to her?

"Do you have a clear policy about cancellations?" I asked her. She said she didn't.

I asked, "Did you explain to Xaviera what your expectations were if she need to cancel?" Again, the answer was no.

"When Xaviera phoned, did you tell her you charge for missed appointments?" No.

When she looked at these answers, my client realized that she is unconscious about money when she doesn't establish clear guidelines and expectations with her own clients.

Laugh

When I do The Work with clients, we frequently dissolve in gales of laughter before we're done. You may be surprised to discover how much fun it is to realize that everything you've complained about is true of you. Rather than being a new way to beat yourself up, The Work frees you to see the glorious ridiculousness that comes from believing our unquestioned thoughts.

Of course, sometimes you won't feel like laughing. You may feel sad as you realize how much energy you have invested in a false belief system or how unfairly you have treated others. That's okay. It is normal to grieve over these realizations. But there is a difference between grief and self-torture.

If you find that you are feeling angry, depressed, or sad, it could be that you've been doing The Work with a motive. I remember a time when I did The Work constantly about a family problem with no results whatsoever. Finally, I realized that I had decided I needed to change in a particular way in order to be happy with the situation. I did The Work over and over, searching for the shift I was sure I needed to make. I never got it.

When we do The Work on our clients or other aspects of business, we may be wanting it to solve a financial problem or relieve our fear of public speaking. While things like this can happen as a side-effect of Inquiry, going in for an express purpose can be very frustrating.

The Work doesn't work when we go in with an agenda. Our hidden motives distort the answers we find for each question. We may act more enlightened than we are or otherwise manipulate our own attitudes and perspectives. The gift The Work delivers is the freedom to live at peace with Reality. To receive that gift, we need to stop trying to predict what Reality should look like.

Getting Paid

Chapter 15

An Elephant Named Money

*Money is like a sixth sense—and you can't make use of
the other five without it. ~Somerset Maugham*

*You can only become truly accomplished at something
you love. Don't make money your goal. Instead, pursue
the things you love doing, and then do them so well that
people can't take their eyes off you. ~Maya Angelou*

Few of us would continue to work for ourselves if it meant
putting money ahead of relationships. Few of us can continue
to work for ourselves unless we make money. Do we have to
choose between making money and being good people?

As accidental entrepreneurs we care about people, quality of
life, beauty, and many other things that we would not trade for
money. Many an accidental entrepreneur affirms this by
declaring, "It's not about the money."

But it is about the money, and then again it isn't. To untangle
that contradiction, let's turn to the story of a feisty locomotive.

The Little Engine that Could

I have always loved the children's story about a train loaded with
toys that was stranded before a huge mountain. Several
impressive engines declined to help, unwilling to exert themselves
on behalf of such trivial cargo. Finally, a little engine succeeded in
pulling the train over the steep pass chanting all the while, "I

think I can; I think I can." The message is that we can accomplish amazing things when we set our sights on the goal and apply sustained effort.

This principle applies in business as well. One of the advantages we have as accidental entrepreneurs is our commitment to the goal and our willingness to work long hours to get there.

But let's remember that no amount of positive thinking would have propelled the train over the hill without fuel.

Fueling the Engine

When you work for yourself, your business has to write your paycheck. The only way it can do that reliably is if you fuel it with money—sometimes with more money than you are used to thinking about. It's not *about* the money any more than driving a car is about the gas or running a train is about the coal, but unless you secure a flow of money to your business, you cannot thrive.

Big Rocks First

Money is an essential building block for the just-right business. Without money, everything else is at risk, just as a house without a foundation is likely to collapse no matter how well the rest of it is built.

In *7 Habits of Highly Effective People*, Stephen Covey tells the story of a professor who brought a large glass jar into her classroom one day. Inside she placed five large rocks.

"Is the jar full?" she asked the class.

There was quite a bit of space around the rocks, so the class said no, the jar wasn't full.

The professor poured a cup of gravel over the rocks as the class watched. "Is it full now?" she asked.

Again, there were gaps between pieces of gravel, and the class said no, the jar wasn't full.

The professor now poured a cup of sand into the jar, filling it to the brim. "Is it full now?"

Most of the class said that it was. Smiling, the professor carefully poured a cup of water over the sand.

The moral is that the way to truly fill our lives is to make room for the big rocks first. For many folks in Covey's audience, that means re-prioritizing in favor of family time, fitness, or spiritual practice. For the accidental entrepreneur, it may well mean giving money more attention and care.

The Elephant in the Living Room

The exchange of money for a product or service is at the very heart of business. No money, no business. Yet for many of us, money is the elephant in the living room, a hulking and inescapable presence that we nonetheless try to ignore.

But money is a store of life energy, and ignoring it has serious consequences, as you'll see in the following case study.

Case Study: Jack and Jill Ignore the Elephant

Jack is a photographer. When Jill asked him if he would be interested in photographing her ceramics, he enthusiastically agreed. He asked what she had in mind and how much she had budgeted. Jill, who had never hired a photographer before, told him she was thinking of spending about $700 but had no idea of how much this kind of work should cost. What did he think it would run?

Jack said his studio rate was $1,200 a day, but he made adjustments for artists. Also, since she was a friend of his wife, Mary, he assured Jill they'd "work something out." Jill was thrilled that such an experienced photographer wanted to shoot her work, and she let go of the subject. They had a great time discussing possible approaches.

A week later, Jill brought her work to Jack's studio. They spent a morning setting up shots, experimenting with lighting and backgrounds. Then Jill asked what he thought about shooting her work in a natural setting. They agreed to meet the next week for a shoot on the beach.

Jack Smith Photography

INVOICE

July 17, 2005

Jill Potter
PO Box 799
Phoenix, AZ 45677

Description	Unit Cost	Total
_ day in studio	$750.00	$750.00
_ day on location	$900.00	$900.00
Processing and retouching	$75.00	$375.00
Sub total		$2025.00
Discount 30%		-$506.25
Total		$1,518.75

Payment is due upon receipt.
Thank you for your business!

999 W. 3rd St. • Phoenix, AZ • 45678 • 989-766-4567 www.joephoto.com

Two weeks later, Jack sent Jill a DVD containing originals of the 20 photos she had selected and 15 images optimized for use on her Web site. He included an invoice for $1,518.75.

Jill was shocked and angry. She had expected to pay $800 or $900, which was more than she had budgeted, but acceptable in order to have Jack do the work.

Jack felt hurt and defensive. He had charged for only a half day each in the studio and on location, in spite of having spent nearly five hours on the first shoot and six on the second. (His usual practice was to charge for a full day whenever he spent more than 5 hours on a project.) He was giving Jill the right to unlimited use of the images, for which he usually charged a hefty additional fee.

In the end, Jill paid Jack $1,000. Both of them felt ill-used, a feeling complicated by the niggling suspicion that they were each responsible for their own misery. Jill spent more than she wanted to. Jack earned less than he felt he deserved. And the relationship is effectively over.

The moral of this story? Ignoring the elephant costs money and relationships.

Application: Talking About Money

Since in this case study both parties are entrepreneurs, we'll apply the Instructions to each of their situations in turn.

Question Stressful Thoughts

What thoughts might Jack have had that kept him from stating a specific fee before accepting the work?

What thoughts might Jill have had that kept her from getting a specific fee before hiring Jack?

Be Yourself

Where do you think Jack's self-image conflicted with being clear about the fee?

Where do you think Jill's self-image conflicted with asking for clarity?

Keep the Channel Open

How might awareness of Source have shifted Jack's inner conversation and outer behavior?

How might awareness of Source have shifted Jill's inner conversation and outer behavior?

Case Study: Should Brian Stick to His Fees?

Sometimes we deal with the elephant in the living room by trying to keep it from upsetting our customers. In other words, we try to prevent them from being troubled by money.

Brian is a former professional racer turned cycling coach. His clients receive weekly individual check-ins, monthly evaluations, personal workouts tailored to their fitness level and goals, and the option of participating in up to four group rides each week. Brian's just-right fee is $550 per quarter, payable at the beginning of each quarter.

Brian came to a coaching session complaining that he had lost his passion for cycling. The work he loved was becoming a grind. After a few questions, Brian revealed that five of his 15 group clients were paying less than his standard fee. I asked if his loss of passion might be related to the loss of income.

At first Brian denied this vigorously. "It's not about the money," he insisted. But when I asked him to imagine how it would be to lead rides and coach folks if every one of his clients was paying the full fee on time and without friction, he admitted that it would feel better. He saw himself being more patient, more attentive, and much more relaxed because he could afford to be fully present.

Still, Brian didn't see how he could get enough business if he stuck to his fee. So we looked at the real contributions and costs related to his reduced fee clients.

Two of his reduced-fee clients were racers who said they couldn't afford the full fee (in spite of earning a good deal more than Brian did at their day jobs). Brian's rationale for charging them less was that their success would be good for his business. (It was certainly good for his self-image.) However, racers were a tiny part of his client base, and given that the racers he did coach had a pattern of asking for price breaks, attracting more racers didn't make a lot of business sense. His rationale for the other three reduced-rate clients was that if he didn't make exceptions, he wouldn't get enough business to survive. Of course, being a cranky and anxious coach was also likely to hurt business.

Brian felt certain that people would resent him and bad-mouth his business if he turned them away because they couldn't pay. We did The Work on the thought, "I turn them away," and Brian realized that the turning away was up to the client, not to him. In other words, what he charges is his business. What people want to pay is there business.

After doing The Work, we did the following role-play. See if you can put yourself in Brian's place as you read it.

Exercise:

In this role-play, I played a prospective client who is very excited about joining Brian's group. Brian played himself. Coaching comments are in italics.

Client: Hi. I'm a friend of Sally's, and she's told me how much she loves riding with you. I've been wanting to get back on the bike myself, and your group sounds perfect for me. What does it cost?
I asked Brian to let my enthusiasm in and to take a moment to experience the pleasure of seeing that I value his work. Then I asked Brian to make eye contact with me and say—

Brian: It's cool that you are so motivated. Thank you for being interested. The cost for the program is $550 a quarter.

Client: *Face falling.* Oh. That's a lot. I guess I can't do it after all.
I asked Brian to maintain eye contact while giving me (the client) room to feel whatever I am feeling without trying to fix it. I invited him to notice what it would be like to stay connected and available to me as he gave the following response—

Brian: That's okay. I understand. And, hey, if your situation changes, I'll be here.

Client: Uh, okay. Thanks.

Imagine yourself in a similar situation in your own business. Play the scene in your mind's eye, watching what happens when you remain connected and available to the other person without trying to manage their emotions or thoughts. Notice stressful thoughts that come up and take them to Inquiry.

Chapter 16

Warning: Contents Under Pressure

Sooner or later just about every accidental entrepreneur feels financial pressure. Your spouse loses his job, your child needs braces, or your accountant announces you made a profit last year ☺ and now you have a hefty tax bill ☹.

Then there are the pressures generated by out beliefs about what money means. An artist believes that if he isn't represented by a major New York gallery he is failure, in spite of being able to pay his bills, travel, and paint. He feels tremendous pressure to sell his work in order to demonstrate its validity. This, in turn, aggravates the internal conflict between being true to his artistic vision and painting what is popular.

Then there is the massage therapist who, after two years—not including training—has a full calendar. She and her husband want to buy a home, but to qualify for a mortgage she will need to increase her prices. Will her friends and clients think she is being greedy? Some of her clients may not be able to afford to pay more. Is it wrong of her to charge them more so she can by a house?

Sometimes we feel the pressure of having too little, sometimes of having too much.

Money Dramas

Money is more taboo than religion or sex. Since the dawn of time, where there is a taboo, there is a drama that defines our relationship to the forbidden fruit. Whether we are conscious of such dramas or not, we are under considerable pressure to live them out so that our worldview remains intact.

In the Authentic Wealth program, we explore a variety of money dramas. The names are tongue-in-cheek, but the plots have very real consequences for our businesses. See if you identify with these:

The Death of a Salesman

Your vision of how things should go isn't working, but it's all you have, so you keep going through the motions. It takes every ounce of energy you have to put a positive spin on things. The better you are at convincing yourself that everything is okay, the more alone and abandoned you feel.

A Streetcar Named Desire

You feel victimized by circumstance and find yourself paralyzed, unable to do anything but nurse your wounded self-image. You keep up appearances as best you can and rely on the "kindness of strangers" to meet your everyday needs.

High Anxiety

Your relationship to money is a rollercoaster ride; sometimes it's up; sometimes it's down. Whatever the current condition, you are constantly anticipating the next move. It's a hoot so long as you keep moving, but if you dare stop, everything comes to a crashing halt.

Gladiator

Money is a battlefield. Sometimes you fight with your partner, sometimes with yourself; at other times the enemy is the tax collector, the utility company, your employer. The names and faces change, but you never run out of reasons to wage war.

The Big Chill

You've made your choices about money, and for the most part they suit you. Sure, you could use more. It would be nice to travel, or contribute to charity, or just take a good long vacation. You harbor some judgments about people who can afford all that and more. Usually, you feel pretty self-satisfied, but sometimes when you look in the mirror you suspect you are selling yourself short by playing it safe.

The Hero's Journey

Dramas are not bad things. Drama is rooted in humankind's earliest attempts to make sense of the mysteries of life and death, not to mention the impenetrable workings of the natural world. At the heart of every drama is the hero's journey. The question is not whether we should have money dramas. The question is whether or not we will take responsibility for the script.

Case Study: Monica's Money Drama

Monica, a nurse who was starting her own business as a patient's advocate with insurance companies, came to a coaching session worried because her husband was leaving his job. "There's a lot of pressure on me to get it together now," she said. "I can't afford to mess around."

Notice how Monica was experiencing pressure: as something external and threatening. There was a "get it together or else" feeling about her drama. Her story had her backed into a corner from which it would be difficult for her to move forward in her business. The more pressure she put on herself, the more confused she got about what to do next.

I asked Monica if she would be willing to play with the possibility that pressure was a gift or an invitation rather than a threat. She agreed.

Subtext

The first thing we played with was subtext, or the underlying sense of the situation. What was the message under the pressure she was experiencing?

Monica readily identified three messages:

I need to get it together, fast.

Time is running out.

I've been relying on him to be the breadwinner for too long.

I asked Monica to imagine that a teacher or other authority figure was giving her these messages because she had done something wrong. When she was ready, I asked three questions, which appear below. Monica's answers are in italics.

1. **How big or small are you compared to whatever is delivering the message?**

   I can't really see whatever it is that is giving me the message. It seems very large, though, like a black cloud.

2. **How close or far from you is the person delivering the message?**

   At first the cloud seemed to be at the other end of the cave—which is where I see us. Then it seemed to get closer and closer.

3. **What are you experiencing in your body as the message is being delivered?**

   First I feel a lot of fear in my belly. I feel almost sick to my stomach. My buttocks and lower back clench, and I start backing up. I feel like I can't breathe. I want to duck, but I am afraid of what might happen if I lose sight of the cloud.

When we were finished with this, I asked Monica to put the phone down and walk around the room, open to whatever might attract her attention. When she noticed something, she should take a moment to pay attention to it whether it was a sound, an object, or even a physical sensation. This is a simple way to for her to make a conscious transition from one state to another.

When Monica came back to the phone, I asked her to close her eyes, relax her belly, and imagine that the pressure she was feeling was a gift, like a blessing a fairy godmother might bestow on a baby princess. She did not need to know why or how it was a gift, just that it was. When Monica said she was ready, I asked her to notice three messages that might be underlying the gift of pressure.

Here's what Monica came up with:

It's your turn to step out.
Trust us. Trust yourself.
This is the first day of the rest of your life.

When she was ready, I asked the same three questions again. Monica's answers are in italics.

1. **How big or small are you compared to whatever is delivering the message?**

   It varies. At first I had the visual of a tiny fairy hovering over a baby. Then it seemed like there were three fairies, but they were life-sized, and I was a grown-up.

2. **How close or far from you is the person delivering the message?**

   Like at my elbow. Near me.

3. **What are you experiencing in your body as the message is being delivered?**

   I feel kind of excited and a little scared. (Here I reminded Monica to notice body sensations.) There's a sort of stirring in my chest, near my heart, and a lot of energy in my belly. I feel quite energetic.

When the subtext changed from criticism to support, Monica experienced the identical pressure in quite different ways. In one instance, the pressure felt punitive, judgmental, and scary. In the other, the pressure was still somewhat scary, but there was also excitement and energy.

We don't have to choose between caving in to pressure or going into defiance or denial. We can be open to the pressure, look for the nurturing and supportive elements that may be in it, and then respond.

Chapter 17
Your Just-Right Price

There's more to setting prices than deciding how much money you need for yourself. If you aren't accustomed to working for yourself you can be blindsided by unanticipated costs. For example, in the USA, you'll pay about 15% in FICA (social security) taxes—twice what you pay when you work for someone else. That's because you are both the employee and employer, so you pay both shares.

Then there's vacation, holiday, and sick pay. These typically add up to four-six weeks in the USA, more in many other countries. True, you aren't required to pay yourself for this time, but your creditors will require you to pay the bills even if you are sick for a week or take a day off.

Let's see. Have I mentioned insurance? Health insurance. Life insurance. Property insurance. Liability insurance. Again, you can choose not to buy insurance policies, in which case you will be responsible for paying the bills yourself. (By the way, I am not an insurance expert. Not everyone needs every kind of insurance. This is an important area in which to ask advice from several sources, preferably not insurance sales people.)

What happens when your computer goes kaput? When the neighbor kid hits a baseball through your office window? As accidental entrepreneurs, we get an up close and personal experience of overhead, taxes, insurance, and other expenses from which we are insulated when we work for someone else.

When you collect a paycheck, it's all yours. Sure, you have bills to pay, but until you pay them, all of your salary or wages are at your disposal. But when you work for yourself, your earnings belong to the business. You get paid (or not) after the needs of the business have been met.

Your business needs to come first for the same reason that grown-ups are instructed by flight attendants to secure their own oxygen masks before assisting their children. Your business cannot serve clients and customers if it is not healthy. And without clients and customers, you don't get paid.

This brings us to the question of how much to charge.

How Much Should You Charge?

According to one school of thought, figuring out how much to charge is a matter of simple addition and subtraction. Add up the costs of doing business, including the cost of paying yourself. Add a margin for contingencies (business-speak for costly  surprises) and profit—say 20%—and divide by the number of billable hours available. If you sell products, the formula is a little different, but the principle remains the same. Charge enough to pay the costs of doing business and make profit.*

It would be irresponsible to charge less than your business needs to pay its bills, so this exercise is worth doing. If you haven't already, please set aside an hour or two (schedule it in your calendar) to add up your business expenses. Schedule another session to add up your personal expenses. Add these two together, tack on another 20%, and you have a pretty good idea of how much your business needs to earn.

---

* Profit is a touchy subject for some of us. Suffice it to say that the root of profit is *proficere*, Latin for "to advance." For our purposes, profit is necessary so that, like all living things, our businesses can grow or advance.

Reality Testing

It may not be realistic to expect your business to earn this much from the beginning. Most businesses don't. To grow a business organically, integrating your personal development with your growth as an entrepreneur, getting to the break- even point can take three years or more.

This means that you'll want to have another source of income while you are growing your business. Your significant other might be the sole breadwinner for a while. You might work part-time. You might draw on savings.

When I closed Mollycoddles, I was very tired of being a drain on our resources. For eight years I had contributed nothing, or so I saw it. Later I came to realize that the years I ran the studio brought many wonderful pieces of art into our home, pieces I acquired by trading with other artists. Because I loved my work (until I didn't), the materials and equipment I purchased for the business were things I would have bought for myself, as I had when I was knitting as a hobby, though the quantity was greater.

Still, in 1996 I wanted nothing more than to start contributing at home. The most important choice I made towards that goal was to go slow.

Going slow made it possible to follow the Three Instructions of The Way of the Accidental Entrepreneur. Whenever I felt I couldn't afford to question my thoughts or take time to keep the channel open—let alone be myself—I would stumble. Sometimes that looked like getting physically ill. More often it looked like spending days or weeks (sad, but true) trying to implement my latest good idea about how to build business, none of which worked.

That's okay. The time I "wasted" going against the flow gave me solid evidence that it didn't work for me. There are faster ways than The Way of the Accidental Entrepreneur to build a business, but I discovered that this is the way I walk. If it's your way, too, accept that. Keep walking and keep your eyes open. Soon you will find the sweet spot where you are respecting yourself, earning a good living, and learning to take better and better care of your business.

Money Isn't Everything

If money were sufficient to provide a great service, rich people would be famous for the caliber of their work. We all know that isn't necessarily the case.

In fact, the only reason money is important at all is that it is the medium of exchange we use to create the inner and outer environments that support our best work.

For example, if you want to deliver work from a spiritual foundation, you need to develop and maintain that foundation. That may means scheduling time for spiritual practice *and doing it.*

I emphasize "doing it" because the accidental entrepreneur is often tempted to sacrifice quality of life in the mistaken belief that working more will result in earning more.

It doesn't work that way. Although there are times when your business will require extra effort, by and large you need to maintain your most important asset: yourself.

This brings us back to money. The time you spend in spiritual practice is time that isn't available for earning income, so you have to charge enough that the hours you do work will cover the hours you don't.

If you want your clients to have the benefit of the latest information and techniques in your field, you need to charge enough to pay for books, training, and conferences.

These are not indulgences. Regardless of what the tax-man says, these are legitimate elements of overhead—the costs of delivering your work.

The Just-Right Price

Whether we have one client or a hundred, there is a price at which we know we can be who we want to be for them without strain, resentment, or depletion. The just-right price is whatever it takes to show up and serve our clients and customers on an ongoing basis.

Exercise: Experiencing "Just-Right"

While it's important to know how much you need to earn, a just-right price isn't something you can "figure out." That's because prices aren't just about money.

The Safe Price

Think about a project you would love to do, something you know you can do well and that you enjoy. Imagine that you are working on this project with a client who is equally committed to the project.

Notice what they need from you and notice how you want to proceed. See yourself doing the work according to the standards that feel just-right to you.

Now, imagine you are charging a "safe" price, not what you want to earn, but what you currently feel you can get away with.

See yourself working on this project for that fee. How do you feel? Do you cut corners or do impeccable work? How do you treat your client both in person and in your mind? How do you treat yourself? How do you feel about working with this person again?

When you have a clear sense of what that would be like, make a few notes.

The Market Price

Shake off the first scenario, then repeat the process, imagining that you are charging the median of your competitors' rates. How do you feel? Do you cut corners or do impeccable work? How do you treat your client both in person and in your mind? How do you treat yourself? How do you feel about working with this person again?

Again, when you have a clear sense of what that would be like, make some notes.

The Right Price

Shake off the previous scenario. Repeat the experiment imagining that you charge the fee you would like to charge.

How do you feel? Do you cut corners or do impeccable work? How do you treat your client both in person and in your mind? How do you treat yourself? How do you feel about working with this person again?

Case Study: Brian's Just-Right Price

Remember Brian the cycling coach? One day he came to a coaching session wanting to "take his business to the next level." In his case, that meant adding another revenue stream. He described three possibilities, and I asked him to imagine he had all the money in the world and tell me which of the three he would do anyway.

"I'd teach people with handicaps how to ride. Man, I just loved working with that little girl last year. Her parents were so excited when they saw her riding in circles in the school parking lot."

Bingo. That told me we were onto the right offer. "Now Brian," I said, "close your eyes and imagine that you are working with a client who has a handicap. Watch yourself and them as you show them how to ride. See yourself showing up exactly the way you want to, fully present, enthusiastic, and patient. Let me know when you have that."

Then I asked Brian to tell me if there was a price that felt "just-right" for the way he wanted to work. He said he knew immediately. "It's $85. Wow. I didn't know that."

I asked Brian if he'd like to test this price, and he agreed. I asked him to keep his just-right situation in mind as I named various hourly rates. I put my own hand on my heart to help me stay connected, and I slowly recited these prices: $45; $70; $55; $65; $90; $50; $85; $70; $75; $60. I mixed up the prices so that

Brian would hear them each individually rather than anticipating increases or decreases.

For Brian, the result was the same. At \$85 per hour he was 100% confident that he would be who and how he wanted to be for his just-right client. By sensing the difference between this price and the other prices, he had an experiential basis for knowing what he needed to charge to do his best work.

Application: The Just-Right Price

It's one thing to arrive at a just-right price, it's another to actually charge it. The three instructions are valuable allies in making the leap.

Keep the Channel Open

As you saw in Brian's story, the just-right price is the price you need to charge to keep the channel open. That is, to be the best channel you can be through which Source can work.

It's not the money, per se, that keeps the channel open. It's the appropriateness of the price both in terms of what you need to earn and what, for lack of a better term, I'll call energetic balance. It takes a certain quality and quantity of life energy to be present for your customers and clients and to deliver the products or services you offer. This life energy cannot be "bottom-lined." We can't read it off a profit and loss statement or balance sheet.

Question Stressful Thoughts

What will he think of me if I ask for that much money?
What if she laughs in my face?
What if she's offended?

These and lots of other thoughts often pop up  when we work with pricing. Sometimes we simply don't believe them. Sometimes we do. When we do, The Work will help us find our truth.

Sometimes we turn to The Work with a motive. We want to prove to ourselves that we are worth our just-right price. We want to reassure ourselves that our clients will accept it. Whatever the motive, it will creep into our answers to the four questions and keep us from experiencing the freedom we're after.

Before you question thoughts about money, you might want to journal about your feelings and fears. Take time to feel the feelings behind your motives. (Motives aren't bad; they just don't work in The Work.) Let yourself notice what it is like to want one outcome or fear another. Then close your eyes and ask your body to show you what freedom feels like. Now you're ready for Inquiry.

Be Yourself

If you're not accustomed to charging the figures that come up when you do the just-right price exercise, it may feel phony, inauthentic, or greedy to charge them. That's a good thing to notice.

When there's a disconnect between your just-right price and the way you see yourself, it will show up in the way you talk to your clients and customers. How could it not, when it is showing up in the way you talk to yourself? If the disconnect feels stressful, listen for the thoughts you are believing, write them down, and take them to Inquiry.

When you ask the third question, "How do I react when I believe that thought? What happens?" pay particular attention to this sub-question: "How do I live my life when I believe this thought?" Take your time as you go in to observe the self that shows up when you believe the thought.

Then, when you to get question four, "Who would I be without this thought?" answer the sub-question, "How would I live my life differently without this thought?" Again, go inside and take your time as you observe the self that shows up without the thought.

Remember, the purpose of doing The Work is not to make yourself comfortable with your just-right price. "Just-right" is a made up concept, one that I hope is useful to you, but not gospel truth. Ultimately, honest self-inquiry is your best guide to what it means to Be Yourself.

Case Study: Andrea's Just-Right Price

The just-right price is closely linked to the just-right work, as you'll see from Andrea's story.

Andrea wants to be a freelance editor, however, she is also able to do technical writing and related work. She asked for my help finding her niche and setting prices. As is often the case, these proved to be so interwoven that we went back and forth between working on the just-right client and the just-right price until the two came together.

We'll pick up Andrea's story at a point where was at a fork in the road when it came to identifying her just-right client. There were several candidates, but no "just-right." So we switched to pricing for a bit, and I asked Andrea to do a variation of what Brian and I did together.

Here's what Andrea has to say about her pricing exercise:

What I found was that at half my desired rate, I felt like I was wasting my time. I like to help people, but I was irritated with myself for not finding customers who would pay me what I think I'm worth. It wasn't a fair exchange. My work was still good, but I didn't give it anything extra, and I felt undervalued by the customer and by myself.

At the rate I want to charge, I found myself excited to do the work, happy to see the customer, more creative and energized.

At a higher fee, it got even better! When I felt, "Wow, I can't believe they're paying me this!" I really had the feeling of how valuable my services were, and I was catapulted into happy, high-performance mode. I also found myself loving my customers and going out of my way to send them creative gifts, take them to lunch, etc.

When Andrea brought this realization to the question of her just-right client, her niche became immediately apparent.

I can see I want to grow my business into a premium service for a premium fee.

This is so helpful! It has me thinking in new directions. Instead of trying to become a top-notch editor, where I don't have all the training and experience, I can be the good editor that I am and focus on helping people clarify and present their ideas in a powerful way. When they are happy with their manuscript, they can choose whether or not to take it to a more specialized editor.

This led me to research book midwife (which turned out to be a trademarked name for a particular writing coach in London) and writing coach. It turns out that "writing coach" is pretty close to what I do, and from what I've been able to find so far, they get paid more than editors, too!

What Is It Worth?

When we have a heartfelt connection to our work, we want more than to get paid. We want to know that our work is valued. This lands us on a slippery slope. It is impossible to control what other people think (darn it all), and the more preoccupied we are about what others think of our work, the less confident we feel.

If we try to compensate for this lack of confidence by looking harder for external validation, we may lose connection with our own values. That makes us even less confident, and we begin to question not only our work but our integrity. Soon we are caught up in a vicious cycle of approval-seeking and self-flagellation.

The way out of this mess is to stop obsessing about what other people think, even when those other people are our customers. Yes, it's important to listen to our customers. It's important to serve them well. And it is a lot easier to do that when we remember that how we value our work is our business and how others value it is theirs.

The Aquamarine Hat

Monsieur Emil was a renowned milliner whose hats were sought by the rich and famous. One day a new customer came to the atelier to commission a hat. She had heard of Monsieur Emil's artistry and she longed to own one of his creations. The milliner accepted her commission, instructing her to return in three weeks.

Three weeks passed and the woman returned for her hat. She waited with bated breath while Monsieur Emil withdrew her hat from its nest of tissue. When he placed the hat on her head and she turned to see her reflection in the mirror, she gasped with delight. A fanciful confection of shimmering aquamarine ribbon, the hat was the most flattering accessory she had ever owned.

Monsieur Emil wrapped the hat carefully, placed it in an elegant hat box, and presented his bill.

The woman's elated expression turned sour as she read the amount: $700. "But this hat is nothing more than ribbon." she objected. "The materials can't have cost ten dollars!"

Monsieur Emil smiled faintly and bowed. Moving with exquisite slowness, he drew the hat from the box and with a few practiced movements reduced the lovely creation to a heap of aquamarine ribbon.

This he handed to his customer, saying calmly, "The cost of the hat, Madame, is $700. The ribbon for free."

Monsieur Emil knew the value of his work *to him*. That is his business. His customer knew the value of his work *to her*. That is her business.

Staying in your business requires regular application of all three instructions. The pay off is that when you are in your business, it is easy for your just-right customers to recognize you and the value your work has for them.

Case Study: The Value of Shining

Angela lives in a wealthy community on the east coast. After getting her Master's degree in Medieval Lit, she married and had kids. Her parents left her a modest trust fund, and while she was raising her children, Angela was fine with being a great mom. Even so, she was active in various community organizations and had a flair for fundraising.

While her kids were in college, Angela got a second Masters' degree, this one in Political Science. She also took a number of communication classes. She thought she'd try speech writing, and she did some work for the state representative from her district. After his re-election, the work dropped off, and she found that she didn't miss it.

Next, Angela trained as a Speaking Circle facilitator. * She held a couple of workshops to rave reviews, nonetheless, business dwindled. About this time Angela also trained as a coach. When she completed her certification, she hired me to help her build a practice.

In the very first session, Angela confessed that she wasn't even sure she wanted a business. I asked her what had drawn her to the fields she had studied. "Shine," she said, "though I know that sounds stupid."

Being a Master Certified Coach, I knew exactly what to say next, and I said it: "Tell me more."†

"I don't know if I can explain it, but I've always had an affinity to showing up—for being visible. It's not about the limelight so much as it is about, well, shining."

"When do you shine?" I asked. After she answered, I asked her to look back at times when she felt she was truly shining. What effect did her shining appear to have on others? How did they react?

---

* Speaking Circles are a the brainchild of Lee Glickstein, author of *Be Heard Now*.

† I'm joking about the significance of my credential, but I am serious about the value of that question. As you coach yourself or work with your support team, listen for the small confessions that have a ring of truth. Invite them out into the open.

Angela realized that when she shined, others blossomed. Not everyone, of course. But certain people opened in remarkable ways both to themselves and others. She didn't have a business model yet, but it was clear that whatever she offered, she was in the business of Shining.

We're still working on the nuts and bolts of Angela's business. What does she need to shine? What kind of schedule? What kind of structure? What kind of clients? And what service can she provide from that shining place?

Now that Angela is clear that the value of her work is in Shining, she is having fun speculating about what her business may look like. So long as she checks her "Shine-Meter" before making decisions, she is almost certain to be on the right track. Whatever she decides to charge her clients, Angela knows her fees have to cover the overhead of Shining because that is the essence of what they want from her.

It's easy to overlook the cost in time, energy, and money of delivering our gifts. If daily meditation, exercise, reading, and gardening, not to mention your weekly French lessons, are what it takes to be fully present, then you have to earn enough to pay for them. Otherwise, you'll be making claims you can't live up to for lack of support.

Application: What's Your Value?

When I began my coaching business my logo was a ladybug and my Web site was coachladybug.com. At the time, the ladybug was my tuning fork. If a choice clashed with "ladybugness" (like taking myself seriously), I invariably found that it dragged me down, even if it was temporarily "good for business."

If something wasn't consistent with "ladybugness," I didn't do it. This was a very subjective test, and it probably wouldn't have worked to decide whether or not to answer the phone. But it was quite helpful when it came to expressing the personality of my business.

Spend a few minutes thinking about what drew you to your work. If you've had more than one career or field of study, get curious about what quality they have in common. Relax, and let the impressions come in their own time.

Keep the Channel Open

When it comes to knowing the value you provide, it's all about how Source is expressed through the unique channel you are. When we get out of the business of judging ourselves, we can appreciate the way we are for what it is: a channel for a greater power.

Be Yourself

Nowhere is this more important than in connecting with the value of your work, and nowhere is it more challenging. The self through which real value flows is often not the self our egos aspire to be.

Question Stressful Thoughts

What thoughts keep you from recognizing and relying on the value of who you are? Here are a few that drop in for tea at my office on a regular basis. As you can see, they are doozies. That makes them perfect for Inquiry. Just make a list of what a stressful thought means, then question each item.

- They won't take me seriously, and that means...
- They'll know I made a mistake, and that means...
- No one is going to pay for ...

Chapter 18

The Art of Asking

Why don't accidental entrepreneurs ask for what we want more often? First, because it doesn't occur to us that we should have to. Isn't it obvious? Second, we don't want to make the other person uncomfortable if she can't or chooses not to comply. And third, we don't want to be disappointed.

Yet, if we are to take care of our businesses (not to mention ourselves), we need to make straightforward requests, preferably without strings attached.

What strings? The strings we attach to protect us from disappointment or disapproval.

Avoiding Disappointment

I don't know about you, but I think about myself all the time. ☺ It's easy to forget that you could be thinking about something else. Another thing—I hate to ask for something unless I know I'll get it. Somewhere along the line I picked up the notion that not getting what you ask for makes you a loser. Yikes!

Put these two characteristics together, and asking clients to pay for products and services gets "interesting."

Of course, there is the real possibility that, if we ask for what we want, people will decline. Fortunately we can learn to ask for what we want and survive whether we get it or not. Just remember that what you want is up to you; whether or not you get it is not.

Strange, but true: It's much easier to ask for what you want if you are willing to hear "no" as an answer. And when you're still afraid of a refusal, you can Question Stressful Thoughts.

Case Study: When a Friend Doesn't Pay

The following is an exchange I had with a reader of my e-zine, *Authentic Promotion*. Natalie was troubled when a client—who also happened to be a good friend—failed to pay a bill.

As you read, put yourself in Natalie's shoes. Work through the situation as if it were happening to you.

> *I was just recently in a situation where I presented a quote to a client, created the marketing materials, and they haven't paid me for my services yet.*
>
> *In addition to this person being my client, she and her husband are like family. I finally sat down and drafted a letter, but still to no avail, no payment. What do you suggest? Should I chalk it up to a loss and stick closer to my business requirements or send out another follow-up letter?*

Notice Your Assumptions

Did you notice that Natalie is assuming that this client doesn't want to pay? Perhaps you agree with her that the fact that she hasn't had a response to her letter is proof that there is a problem. But is that true?

Suppose you had a terrific lasagna the last time your friend had you over for dinner, and she promised to give you the recipe. You're having company this weekend and you want to serve lasagna. But it's been three weeks, and she hasn't sent you the recipe.

Would you imagine that she was lying when she promised to give you the recipe? Would you worry that calling her might endanger your friendship? Actually, I have to admit that I have occasionally been that crazy. But for the sake of our example, let's assume that we realize that our priorities are not always shared, even by people who love us.

Sometimes it takes The Work to get to a place of neutrality from which we can know the next step. (She doesn't want to pay me. Is it true? Can I absolutely know that it is true?) Sometimes just remembering that we are not the center of someone else's universe is enough to show us the way.

Living the Turnaround

In this case, let's assume Natalie has done The Work on "She doesn't want to pay me." She's found these juicy turnarounds:

She does want to pay me.
I don't want to pay her.
I don't want to pay me.

When Natalie looks for ways each turnaround might be as true or truer than the original thought, she discovers:

She does want to pay me. *This could be truer. After all, she asked for the work and she accepted my estimate. She has not complained about the work or said anything to indicate that she doesn't want to pay. Her silence could be embarrassment at not being able to pay yet or simply having other things on her mind.*

I don't want to pay her. *Oh yes. I don't want to pay her the compliment of assuming she wants to pay me. I don't want to pay attention to this, and that's like not wanting to pay attention to her and our relationship. I don't want to find out that she has a complaint about the work, in which case I might have to "pay her" by adjusting the bill.*

I don't want to pay me. *Very true. I would prefer to not have to ask again. I don't want to pay me the time and effort it may take to collect this money. I also don't want to pay me by letting go of it and getting back the energy and enthusiasm this is draining.*

Having really sat with these turnarounds, Natalie was ready to call her friend and client from a neutral place, without her stories about what might be wrong. Here's how I suggested Natalie proceed from there.

> *Before you call, imagine that she has every intention of paying you. After all, you can't know that she doesn't. Take a moment to get calm and centered.*
>
> *Ask if she has a minute. Assuming she does, let her know you are calling to see if she is satisfied with the work you did.*
>
> *Then wait as if you are truly interested and curious. Listen with your full attention to the answer. Avoid defending, explaining, or justifying. Concentrate on hearing her.*

Asking Without Strings

When your client lets you know that they feel you fully understand their position, it's your turn to ask for what you want. Here are some of the tips I gave Natalie for this step.

> *Odds are that your client has no complaint about the work. In that case, you can say, "I wanted to make sure. I haven't received your check, so I thought maybe there was a problem."*
>
> *Again, wait for her to respond. Maybe she never received the invoice. She may have been too embarrassed to let you know that cash was tight. She may have left the bill and reminder letter in a stack on her desk and forgotten them. (I used to think that was nonsense, then I turned 50 and forgot all kinds of things I didn't believe a person could lose track of.)*
>
> *After she has said what she has to say, make your request, whatever that may be. Some examples:*
>
> *I'm so glad that there isn't a problem. May I drop by and pick up a check tomorrow?"*
>
> *"I'm glad to know that it's just that you are waiting for a client to pay you. I was counting on the check. Can you pay me half now and half in 30 days?"*

Example: When the Client Is Dissatisfied

Essentially, the steps are the same regardless of whether or not your client was satisfied. Inquire, listen, verify that you understand, and ask the next indicated question until you agree on a resolution.

That can be hard to imagine if you are feeling vulnerable. Here's one possible scenario to show you how the conversation might unfold.

Client: Actually, I didn't want to say anything, but our printer had a lot of trouble with the art. I don't understand the details, but it was quite a hassle.

You: That sounds frustrating. I'd like to talk to your printer to find out what happened. Would that be all right with you?

Client: Well. I don't know. He's pretty busy.

You: I understand. It sounds like you don't want to add to the hassle he's already had.

Client: He already thinks I'm the customer from Hell.

You: Yikes! Now I'm really curious about what happened.

Client: Beats me. I just know it delayed the job and he wasn't very happy about it.

You: Here's what I'd like to do. I'd like to call the printer and find out what happened. Then I can call you back and we can talk about settling the account. How does that sound?

Client: Okay, I guess.

You: Super. I'll get back to you ASAP. By the way, who is your printer?

The key to this conversation is to remember that the truth—whatever it may be—is not a problem. Monitor your internal dialogue and let go of your stories. Keep your focus in the present moment.

Inquiry: Asking for More

What if you'd like to raise your prices but you're hesitating because you are afraid your clients will leave? As you read the following Inquiry, go inside and find your own answers.

My clients will leave if I raise my prices.

Is it true?

If your answer is yes, ask question 2: **Can I absolutely know it's true that my clients will leave if I raise my prices?** Whatever your answer to that, go on to question 3: **How do I react when I believe that thought? What happens?** Go inside and watch how you treat your clients and yourself when you believe the thought. Notice how your body reacts. Take your time. You may discover something like this:

> *When I believe that thought I feel heavy and tired. It's hard to get excited about work. I love my clients, but with this thought I feel as if they are draining my energy sometimes. I worry about how I can lead a workshop if I can't afford to print a decent workbook. I get cranky and inattentive because I don't take enough time for rest and recreation.*

> *I treat myself like a workhorse. I drive myself to do more for more clients so that I don't have to raise my rates in order to earn more. I tell myself I can't risk rejection. I treat myself like I am needy and inept.*

> *I feel sadness in my face and eyes. My mouth and throat are tight. So is the back of my neck. I want to run away and hide.*

Now it is time for question 4: **Who would I be without the thought?** Again, go inside and watch how you treat yourself and your clients when you drop your story. Just watch who you are and how you show up when you don't have that thought. You may find something like this:

> *Without the thought that my clients will leave, I see myself telling a client about my new prices and staying present to them. Instead of pulling back and putting on a shell to protect me from their anger or disappointment, I feel very connected and present. I really care about them, and I care whether or not they choose to pay the new price. I am peaceful.*

Finally, turn the thought around. Look for the opposites of your thought, then go in and ask: "Is this as true or truer than my original thought?"

My clients will leave me if I raise my prices turns around to:

My clients will not leave me if I raise my prices. *This is as true. For all I know none of them will leave me.*

My clients will leave me if I don't raise my prices. *This is truer. If I don't raise my prices I could become more and more resentful and confused. That's not very attractive to my clients, and it gets in the way of doing good work.*

I will leave my clients if I don't raise my prices. *Absolutely truer. I leave my clients when I charge less than I need to in order to make a profit and continue to be of service. I've also left them a hundred times in my thoughts—whenever I thought about raising prices.*

I will leave me if I raise my prices. *Ooh. Yes, I see how this is truer. I will "leave me" if I raise my prices so much or so rapidly that I feel disconnected from myself.*

Case Study: What Should You Ask For?

Margo is an artist who wants to be recognized in the context of a sophisticated artistic community and regular, frequent interaction with artists, reviewers, and art patrons. When I asked her whom she could ask for help, she said she didn't even know what to ask for.

When we consider the whole of what we want, asking for it can feel way too risky, not to mention dumb. If you wanted to buy a house for the first time, you probably wouldn't walk into a bank and say, "Oh, Mr. Loan Officer, will you please give me a $500,000 loan?" But if you chunk it down, you can find lots of things you can ask for, like help interpreting your credit report. If you don't know how to chunk down the big picture, ask for help doing that.

Margo knew what she wanted in terms of the big picture, so I asked her what she thought she needed to make that picture real. For example, here's how she broke down her desire for being part of a peer group.

To connect with creative peers, I can:

- Make a list of the qualities I want in a peer.
- Attend openings and gallery walks. When I see work I like, ask about the artist.
- Ask people if they know anyone who might know anyone who knows a person I want to meet.
- Check out online communities.
- Visit the arts council office and see what they have to offer
    o Events
    o Networking
    o Public art
- Be visible
    o Press releases
    o Send postcards or e-cards of my work

Then I asked Margot to think of something she could ask for related to each item on her list. Her answers are in italics.

- Make a list of the qualities I want in a peer.
Ask Linda to help me. She knows me better than anyone else.

- Attend openings and gallery walks. *Make a date with someone for at least one event a week.*

- When I see work I like, ask about the artist. *Ask my companions to support me in this.*

- Ask people if they know anyone who might know anyone who knows a person I want to meet. *Ask Linda and Barry to help me by asking folks they know, too. Ask my coach to hold me accountable for following through each week.*

- Check out online communities. *Call the library reference desk and ask for guidance. Call the museum office and ask for suggestions. Ask the arts council people, too.*

- Visit the arts council office and see what they have to offer:

  o Events. *Let them know that I am interested in meeting other artists.*

  o Networking. *Ask for help contacting reviewers, curators.*

  o Public art. *Ask to volunteer for the review committee*

- Be visible.

  o Press releases. *Ask library reference desk about media contact info; call papers and magazines and ask what their deadlines are.*

  o Send postcards or e-cards of my work. *Ask the arts council if they have resources to help artists publicize their work; ask about graphic designers in the area..*

For additional insight into what you want, see Chapter 8, Keep the Channel Open, especially the Instrument Rules practice on page 62. See also Goals That Fit Just-Right on page 7 and the sections on Desire, page 65, and Passion, page 66.

Chapter 19

Open the Tap

For years I conspired to keep myself living in what I thought of as genteel poverty because I thought it made me a good person. More accurately, I thought it *protected* me from being a bad person. Righteousness and fear kept me small and anxious. Other people's needs were a threat because, after all, I barely had enough for myself. Every day I gathered evidence that there is not enough to go around.

One day I realized I had my hand on the tap. I was keeping the flow of material prosperity to a trickle. Sure, external circumstances influenced how much I earned, but the one controlling how much of the available prosperity flowed in, through me, and out again was me. I resolved to open the tap wide.

When I realized that I had been restricting the flow of well being, I also realized I could expand it. That's not an overnight job, but why not expand our capacity for joy, compassion, wealth, pleasure, and support?

How Does Your Garden Grow?

In the first years of my coaching business, my husband and I lived in a wonderful old farmhouse with a large yard. I wanted to grow flowers, and I decided to plant a perennial garden.

There was no telling how long we would live in the house or even how long it would remain standing. The property was slated for development, and we were renting until the parcel sold.

This led to the most satisfying gardening experience I've ever had. I realized that whatever I put into the garden—seeds, bulbs, bushes, fertilizer, time, and love—had to be given without expectation of any return. If I wanted satisfaction, I needed to find it in the moment.

I will always be grateful for that experience because it taught me that it is possible to plan, invest, and create without attachment to results. We don't need to be dissatisfied with what we have in order to open ourselves to the possibility of more. As creative beings, it is in our nature to imagine and even invest in the future. We can be fully satisfied now when we plant seeds for the future.

Be Rambunctious

When our grandchildren visit they run to Grandpa, hollering, "Let's go upstairs and be rambunctious!" Being rambunctious looks like jumping on the bed while throwing yoga balls. (I'm not invited because I get nervous when large objects are thrown indoors, and that puts a damper on rambunctiousness.)

Rambunctiousness is a wonderful way to open the channel to Source and to tap into the excitement of a hero's quest. When we're rambunctious, desire and creativity pull out all the stops. Every business needs a little time to be rambunctious.

Exercise: Rambunctious Desire

Make a list of 101 things you want.

That's it. You may be able to get to 101 in an hour, or it could take weeks. As you think about what you want, invite all of your senses to participate. Approach your list like a game of make believe where there are no limits. Then put your list in a special place: inside a treasured book, in a pretty vase, under your pillow. When you need a little rambunctious energy, pull it out and see what you can work toward here and now.

The Boss of the Universe

As you make the list, you may notice a thought like this: "I shouldn't tell the Universe what to give me." That's interesting. One minute you are making a list, the next you are in cosmological tug-of-war.

Then again, you might be making your list when you notice a thought like this: "I wonder if I forgot to turn off the sprinkler."

The point is that thoughts pop up independent of our wills. That a thought appears is not a big deal. The big deal (if there is one) happens when we believe the thought even when it argues with reality. By the way, I certainly hope that you aren't thinking of a purple elephant in a yellow bikini in the bathroom.

When you read that sentence, you didn't get to choose whether or not to think a thought of a purple elephant in a yellow bikini in the bathroom. The thought appeared with the words. It's a goofy thought, and believing there is a purple elephant in a yellow bikini in the bathroom could be stressful. But because you don't believe it, the thought is free to float away to wherever it is that thoughts go when we let them.

I invite you to notice any stressful thoughts that come up as you make your list of 101 things you want. Jot them down on a separate piece of paper and take them to Inquiry. (That is, if they don't float away first.)

Giving Back

One of the most exciting things that can happen to an accidental entrepreneur is to be invited to donate products or services to a good cause. Not only do these requests validate your work, they give you a chance to be generous, and being generous can feel a lot like being rich.

At the same time, requests for donations can create confusion and resentment. If you give beyond your means, you may cripple your business, impeding or even closing down the channel through which you are able to serve.

Rather than waiting until you are asked to make a donation, why not choose a cause or an organization that you would love to support. Make a plan for how you can contribute, whether by giving time, offering your expertise, or donating to an auction or other fundraiser.

This way you get to choose how you give back. When you are asked to make donations outside of your chosen focus, you can explain that you already have a giving plan. If you want to consider making additional donations in the future, keep a file of requests to review at the end of the year when you review your plan.

To Discount or Not to Discount

In addition to responding to requests for donated or reduced fee services, you may be wondering whether to offer reduced prices or even give work away. Before you make any decisions about reducing your fees, bartering, or offering pro bono services, sit with the following questions.

What do you want to give?
What results do you want from giving?
When has giving been effortless?
When has giving been a problem for you?

Giving in accordance with your deepest desires, resources, and needs is energizing, motivating, inspiring. It is relatively easy to make a sustained contribution when you truly care about a cause and have adequate resources. It is relatively easy to deliver quality products and services at a discount when you are meeting the needs of your business.

And it is remarkably easy to become resentful and depleted when we give more than we really can. Use the following exercise to look more deeply at what to give and how.

Exercise: Who, What, When, and How of Giving

Examine your commitments, noticing especially where you might feel resentful or anxious. What is behind this resentment or anxiety? Have you given more than you can afford from available resources? Do you have expectations, monetary or otherwise, that have not been met?

There are many forms of compensation besides cash. How would it feel if you were to give your services in exchange for specific and authoritative feedback? Is there an opportunity for barter? If you barter, how will you measure the respective value of the goods and services being exchanged?

If you were only concerned with how responding to a request might *feel,* and not with how it might *look,* what decision would you make? How would it be to utterly trust yourself to make the decision that works for you?

As you ask these questions, allow the answers to arise without criticism or censorship. Know that letting yourself be honest about what you do and do not truly value will help you to make stronger commitments, commitments that you will love to keep and that will serve others.

Context

Context is the setting or circumstances that give events and communications meaning. If you're walking down the street in a business suit and someone runs up and dowses you with a bucket of water, it's an assault. If you're in the locker room after winning a soccer game, getting dowsed with water is a celebration.

In Chapter 9 we looked briefly at the role of money in differentiating business and social contexts. In the context of business it is not only okay to make choices based on money, it is essential. When we say, "It's not about the money," we are really saying, "I'm not doing business."

Of course, it isn't *only* about the money. It's also about relationships. Our work, then, is to consciously cultivate a context for getting paid that is business-like (respects the role of money) and generous (honors Source and blesses others).

Generosity is the quality of giving more than is strictly expected or required. When we give generously, we feel a certain largeness, as though we have stepped into a grander story.

Sourcing Generosity

True generosity flows from an ample Source. The key to being generous is to realize that you are not that Source, but that you are a channel through which that Source flows to others. That means that the first requirement for generosity is to Keep the Channel Open.

You don't need to be extravagant or irresponsible to be generous. In fact, when you work for insufficient fees or give away time and resources that are needed for a healthy business, you may be getting in the way of the flow for yourself and your customers and clients.

Whether you are a Pagan, a Jew, an Atheist, or a cradle-Catholic with Buddhist leanings like me, you've experienced some power greater than yourself. You aren't responsible for how much or how little comes through the channel, only for keeping the channel open.

Grace

The power that flows from Source is freely given, gratis, that is, by grace. We don't (and can't) earn it or own it. This can be a problem for the parts of us that want to be important or take credit. It's also a problem for the parts of us that think we need to know what can't be known, like what will happen next.

Fortunately, it is not necessary to understand Source to receive grace. It's likely if that mom had stopped to think before lifting the car, she would have failed. When we try to figure out what Source is and how to get more grace, awareness of our own limitations breeds doubt and suspicion. Not wanting to be naïve or irresponsible, we cut ourselves off from what we most need.

Short of perfect enlightenment, whatever that is, our experience of Source is usually episodic and unpredictable. It is important for us to understand and accept this so that we don't beat ourselves up for the time we spend disconnected and disconsolate. To do business from a context of generosity means doing our best to maintain conscious connection with Source and forgiving ourselves when we fall short of the mark.

Willingness to Receive

Like water, grace flows toward the lowest point along the line of least resistance, without experiencing the least discouragement when it meets obstacles even of stone or steel. An unfailing means of restoring or increasing connection with Source is to allow ourselves to become that low point, trusting to the penetrating power of grace to cut through apparent obstacles including our own resistance.

Of course, this takes us out of the holiness business, if by holiness we mean possessing an open line to Source. True receptivity means letting go even of our desire to be more receptive! In a word, we need to be needy.

This is a kind of abandoned neediness, a hopeless neediness that has given up searching for relief. This is neediness beyond whining or grasping. And the surprising thing is that it feels really good once we get there.

It is a tremendous relief to throw up our hands and say, "Okay, You do it!" to the God of our understanding. "Let me know when it's my turn to do something, Big Guy. And by the way, don't be subtle. I'm not in the mood for hints."

Throw in a few choice expletives, if you like. It works for me every time.

Abundance

Abundance is a concept. It means different things to different people. It can even mean different things to the same person on different days. In my book, that makes it a crummy measure of spiritual accomplishment in spite of all the happy talk to the contrary.

I get angry when I read some self-styled spiritual business guru hold forth on how his millions prove the efficacy of his unique, spiritually-based system of building a business. It's not just that I have spent umpteen dollars buying those systems only to find out that they are thinly veiled sales vehicles for yet another system, technique, or "insider secret." It's that every week I hear from people who believe that if only they believe the right thing in the right way, they will be rich.

This isn't a get-rich-quick book, but I can tell you how to be rich right now. Close your eyes. Surrender to gravity. Let the surfaces below you and below them support you. Just for now, let go of trying to be or do anything. Drink in the wellbeing of this moment. There it is: abundance. You are rich.

But hey, when you open your eyes, the light bill is still there, right in front of you. Your computer is still slow, and you haven't taken a real vacation since you started to work for yourself. I won't blame you if the reality of abundance seems, well, theoretical.

Abundance is the state of having more than enough, and this means that abundance turns on the question: "What is enough?"

Allow me to suggest that enough is what it takes to be grateful, that gratitude is how we know we have enough. You can test this by keeping a gratitude journal. Write five things you are grateful for every morning and five more every evening. Pause when you write and let yourself really feel your gratitude. In that moment, can you honestly say you don't have enough?

Until we experience the abundance of simple existence, we are going to experience ourselves as needy, and it is darn hard to attract income as an entrepreneur if you feel and act needy. I've tried it.

In my experience, abundance became available when I combined two things:

1.   The realization that I already had plenty (another word for abundance and another word for enough).

2.   The permission to want more.

There is no inherent conflict between the realization that we have enough and the permission to want more. As far as I know, wanting more is human nature. When we unhook the pure fun of wanting from the tortured hallucination that we don't have enough, wanting is simply creativity at play.

Afterword

There will come a time when you believe everything is finished. That will be the beginning. ~Louis L'Amour

So where do you go from here? Back to the beginning, of course, or to a chapter or exercise that grabbed your attention. What matters is that you keep on walking.

It's a lot easier to see a business from outside, and you will learn a tremendous amount both from your ability to help another entrepreneur and from their ability to help you. Form a study group. Join Shaboom County (described below). Take a class. Just be sure that you meet regularly with other accidental entrepreneurs.

Apart from that, I offer this short list of implications of self-employment as a spiritual path. In my experience, they hold true whatever your spiritual tradition and beliefs.

1. We are each responsible for the value of our own work and for how it is perceived in the world. The value that clients and customers place on our work is not likely to exceed the value we place on it.

2. Prosperity is directly related to our priorities. It is up to each of us to be clear about what prosperity mean and to make attaining those things a priority.

3. Prosperity is directly related to expectations. When we expect the best, we make the most of each opportunity, including the opportunities disguised as disappointments.

4. The experience of success and failure is directly related to our fundamental expectations about life. If we believe that things generally go wrong, they will.

5. Marketing is an inside job. When we know what we do, love what we do, and are willing to tell those who may benefit what we do, marketing is natural, effortless, and sustainable.

6. The best attitude in the world is insufficient without action. Results happen when we walk our talk.

7. When we are in our own business, we bless everyone around us. The more on purpose and prosperous we are, the more those blessings seed purpose and prosperity for others.

8. Adversity is an invitation to laugh at and learn from our mistakes.

9. Our work is a gift. When we trust that more will be given, we can surf the shifting tides of success and apparent failure with grace and good humor.

10. When we are willing to know what we want and to ask for it without strings, we always to get it or something of even greater value.

Steppingstones

With this book, you have what you need to begin the journey toward a business that fits just-right. Read it. Work the exercises. Apply the Three Instructions to the challenges you face from day to day. And when you are ready for the next step, you'll find it in Shaboom County.

Shaboom County is an online community for accidental entrepreneurs. Every member will have and be using this book. In time members will be able to download worksheets and exercises from this book as well as free e-books and other useful business tools.

The heart of the County is the Town Hall, an online discussion forum where members can request and receive support form each other and from me. I'll be spending 5-10 hours per week building the community, and a substantial portion of that will be responding to the requests of members.

There are lots of other goodies in the planning stages. I hope your voice will be among those that shape things to come.

As of this writing, Shaboom County is in beta testing. We're planning to roll it out gradually throughout 2008. Updates about Shaboom County will appear in my weekly e-zine, *Authentic Promotion.* You can also email maggie@shaboominc.com for more information.

I hope I will "see" you there.

Appendix
Finding Stressful Thoughts

O ddly enough, it can be difficult to identify stressful thoughts even when we are stuck and unhappy. For my part, I often repress my stressful thoughts because I don't want to believe that I believe them. But that doesn't make the little buggers go away. Sometimes I think that stressful thoughts hide because they know that, if they show up, I will attack. How dare they lower my evolution quotient?

If for any reason you draw a blank when it comes to finding a stressful thought, answering these questions and completing the sentence stems should reveal a bunch of concepts to take to Inquiry. Think of your answers as a bucketful of wriggly earthworms just begging to be used as bait. ☺

How could you life be better than it is now?

What do you wish were different?

What is in your way?

Who do you envy?

Who do you resent?

What do you fear?

What would make things easier?

What's wrong with _____?

Bibliography

*H*eaven forfend. Sister Somebody-or-other would be appalled at the lack of formal citations. Oh well! Google the titles and authors and/or check your local library or bookstore and I am certain you will find what you need.

Applied Kinesiology, Robert Frost

Attracting Perfect Customers, Stacey Hall, Jan Brogniez

The Book of Hours, Rainer Maria Rilke, trans. Joanna Macy

The Brain Audit, Sean D-Souza

Brain Gym for Business, Gail E. Dennison, et al

The E-Myth, Michael Gerber

The Essential Rumi, Coleman Barks

Good to Great, Jim Collins

How to Meditate, Lawrence Le Shan

Loving What Is, Byron Katie Mitchell

Made to Stick, Chip Heath and Dan Heath

The Power of Focusing, Ann Cornell Weiser

The Power of Full Engagement, Jim Loehr, Tony Schwartz

7 Habits of Highly Effective People, Stephen Covey

Wishful Thinking, A Theological ABC, Frederick Buechner

About the Author

You know how some people's lives seem to follow a nice clean trajectory? Not mine. My road kind of disappeared when I was 17 and my dad died, leaving my mom with eight children, of which I was the eldest.

Overnight, our storybook family turned into a poster-family for dysfunction and disaster. My mom and siblings moved to San Francisco; I moved to Seattle.

Between the ages of 18 and 21 I learned to wait tables, serve cocktails, and manage an office. I also learned to party, which given my over-responsible childhood, served as a reasonable facsimile of play.

The Love Interest

In 1974 I met and fell in love with Miles Yanick. I became manager of his architectural firm, and, thanks to the Boeing recession, got a rapid and thorough education in business management during hard times.

The Plot Thickens

Life went on. I worked hard and partied harder. I went back to college, almost completing my junior year before partying became a full time endeavor. In 1984, I entered rehab, and began graduate studies in life, the universe, and everything.

Grad School

I threw myself headlong into recovery, learning everything I could about addictions. I devoured books on psychology and spirituality and learned to see myself clearly, even when it wasn't pretty.

Over the next five years I had a variety of jobs, each of which added a piece to my crazy quilt resume. From word-processing to business planning to editing and layout, I gathered the skills that would one day make Shaboom a reality.

Skating on Thin Ice

In 1987 my lifelong fascination with knitting and sewing had spawned a part-time business creating wearable art. By 1989, we were out of debt, though by no means on easy street, so I did the logical thing.

I quit my job and opened Mollycoddles, a wearable art studio. (At the time I owned a 1967 Volkswagen Beetle, so, of course, I made a "vest" for it.)

Self-employment proved to be the most challenging path I had ever walked. I made every mistake a person could make, and then went on to make some more.

Today, those mistakes, along with the rest of my checkered resume, are my primary qualifications for showing accidental entrepreneurs how to build businesses that fit just right.

Believe me, if I can do it, so can you.

From Wearable Art to Artful Living

In 1995 I closed Mollycoddles and started saying "yes" to people who, without encouragement from me, had been asking me to help them manage and market their small businesses.

I didn't know I was a coach until one of my first clients sent me a Newsweek article about Thomas Leonard, a pioneer in the field, with the note, "This is what you do."

When I found out about coaching, I could hardly believe what I saw. It was as though someone had designed a profession for which my "portfolio" past had been the perfect training.

Life Could Be a Dream...

Thanks to my checkered past, I'm able to draw road maps for other accidental entrepreneurs—people who love their work enough to risk working for themselves but who aren't particularly business oriented and who have a deep commitment to personal growth.

I love that everything I learn (and every mistake I make) serves this audience. From The Work of Byron Katie to Embodied Intelligence, ontological coaching to Process Work to integral theory and methodology, there is delicious synergy among my vocation and avocations.

These days TCP (aka Miles, aka The Charming Prince) and I live in Suquamish, Washington, with Bolivia the wonder cat and three hens: Viola Swamp, Miss Nelson, and Daisy Belle. We are blessed with two astonishing grandchildren (not to mention their parents), who live in nearby Seattle.

Molly